My Walk in
June

Shannon Savage

WestBow
PRESS®
A DIVISION OF THOMAS NELSON
& ZONDERVAN

WestBow Press books may be ordered through booksellers or by contacting:

WestBow Press
A Division of Thomas Nelson & Zondervan
1663 Liberty Drive
Bloomington, IN 47403
www.westbowpress.com
1 (866) 928-1240

Scripture quotations marked (NIV) are taken from the Holy Bible, New International Version®, NIV®. Copyright © 1973, 1978, 1984, 2011 by Biblica, Inc.™ Used by permission of Zondervan. All rights reserved worldwide. www. zondervan.com The "NIV" and "New International Version" are trademarks registered in the United States Patent and Trademark Office by Biblica, Inc.™

Scripture quotations marked (NLT) are taken from the Holy Bible, New Living Translation, copyright ©1996, 2004, 2015 by Tyndale House Foundation. Used by permission of Tyndale House Publishers, Inc., Carol Stream, Illinois 60188. All rights reserved.

ISBN: 978-1-9736-8508-1 (sc)
ISBN: 978-1-9736-8507-4 (hc)
ISBN: 978-1-9736-8509-8 (e)

Library of Congress Control Number: 2020902619

Print information available on the last page.

WestBow Press rev. date: 02/11/2020

With overwhelming love and a full heart, this
book is dedicated to Zane and Xavier.

The two of you are the true loves of my life. May you
always know that your earthly father, who now resides in
heaven, loved you beyond words on earth and loves you
still in heaven. May you always know that you also have a
heavenly Father, who loves you without end and will hug
your earthy father for you. All you need to do is ask.

For God has not given us a spirit of fear and timidity,
but of power, love, and self-discipline.

—2 Timothy 1:7 (NLT)

CONTENTS

FOREWORD

This book is not written by a theologian. But it contains excellent theology. It is not written by a grief counselor. But it contains helpful and practical insights into what the journey of grief is like. It is not written by a Bible scholar. But it is filled with many scriptural references appropriately applied.

My Walk in June is written by a friend of mine whose life was literally tossed upside down in a minute but with lifelong consequences. She was thrust onto a roller coaster ride on which she didn't want to be and for which she certainly did not buy a ticket. Her stagnant faith was stretched beyond comprehension, but rather than break apart, it has strengthened immeasurably. When she wanted to run away from the grief, she instead ran into it and faced it head-on. When she thought she had a handle on all of this, her hands were ripped off, and she spiraled downward in a free fall, only to discover that God's strong hands were still holding her.

As Shannon's pastor before, during, and after the events of June 6, 2010, I've been privileged to have a front-row seat to much of what she shares. I've seen the raw, messy reality of which she writes. And I so admire the courage and integrity with which she tells it. She doesn't hide behind a plastic Christian façade; she recounts the journey as she has lived it: in awe of God, cursing God, trusting God, questioning God, and, always, held by God. That is where the true value of this book resides. That is where the faith and life lessons for us can be found.

My prayer is that none of you who read this will ever have to live anything like it. But some of you will. And many more of us will face the reality of journeying with a friend through a major crisis point in his or her life. The insights of this book will be most helpful as they too find themselves on an emotional and spiritual roller coaster ride from which they can't get off. I'm so grateful that Shannon has had the courage to share with us what normal is like in those moments and days and months when nothing is normal.

Pastor Don

PREFACE

Writing for me started out as personal therapy. It was a way for me to sort through my own thoughts and release anger, pain, and even hope. I started to share bits and pieces of my raw and real feelings through social media outlets. The more I did, the more I felt some relief. As God was revealing Himself and His truths to me, I became increasingly bold in sharing my faith. Suddenly, I didn't care if people thought I was a crazy Jesus person. All I knew was that I was seeing, feeling, and understanding God in a way that I never had before. I wanted people to experience what I was starting to experience. As time went on, I began to receive feedback and messages from others thanking me for being so open and so real about my journey. My faith was becoming an encouragement to others, and I liked being able to help others. I started to see that the tragedy of Mark's death was going to be used to help others through whatever tragedy their lives would entail. I started to realize that people were watching me as I started to navigate through this horrible ordeal. Was I going to be open and real with hope, faith, and strength, or was I going to be a victim? I never wanted to be a victim and never wanted to be a super-Christian either. I wanted to show people that having a real faith in Jesus Christ is just as much about breaking, questioning, and falling away from faith as it is about worshipping, praising, praying, and believing wholeheartedly.

I was often asked when I going to write a book. I would laugh it off, but writing a book was becoming something I seriously contemplated. It's been a process. A nine-year process in fact. The first four or five chapters of *My Walk in June* have been written now for about five years. It might sound crazy, but God woke me up in the middle of the night one time about five years ago with random phrases going through my head. I realized that He was giving me the book title and chapter titles. He was giving me direction as to what He wanted in the book because I had no idea where to start. I wrote the phrases down, and that is when *My Walk in June* truly began.

I'm reminded of King David. He was only a ten-year-old boy when he was anointed by Samuel to become king of Israel. David did not actually become king until decades later. He had a whole lot of life to live before God's calling of him as king became a reality. David would make a lot of mistakes, commit a lot of sin, ask for a lot of forgiveness, and live out a lot of humanness before he would become king. God started something in David when he was only ten. He didn't finish what He started with David until he was a man. God's plans don't come to completion until He says so. I feel as if it's the same with me writing this book. He put the idea of writing a book in my head eight years ago. Just like David, there were a lot of mistakes I had to make, a lot of sins I had to commit, and a lot of repentance I had to do. There were new experiences I had to encounter. I needed to endure new hardships and learn more about myself and about God before the book was written. Yes, it is true that the idea of writing a book was put into my head shortly after Mark died, but this book is just now becoming a reality, almost a decade after Mark died.

My point is that if God puts an idea in your head, and it doesn't seem to be going anywhere, be patient. He may just be growing you until the time is right to bring that plan to fruition. Despite David being an adulterer, a murderer, and many other things, he was still a man after God's heart. God knew his heart. David would sin greatly and then sincerely cry out to God in repentance. God still used him. He still used such a messed-up and broken human being for something as tremendous as king of Israel. God knows our hearts too. He will use the most scarred and beaten-down people to accomplish great things. Do I dare to believe that He wants insignificant me to write a book? Do you dare to believe that He wants you to do something amazing too?

I admit that I'm a little reluctant and scared to tell my story. I'm not entirely sure why. I suppose it's because I fear judgment. I fear mocking. I fear it's not good enough. I fear failure. It's overwhelming and scary to think that I am basically putting my life of the past ten years out there for anyone to read. I question if I want people to know the depths of my being. Then I remember that I am a child of God and that I don't need to fear. Fear is not from God. It's from the enemy; therefore, I am stronger than my fear. I also believe my desire for people to know just how difficult but beautiful my journey has been trumps any fear I may feel. People need to know that being a single mother due to the death of a spouse is daunting. It's something that one will never get over. Not even ten years later. People need to know that it can come back at any time even worse than it was at the beginning. People need to know it's something that never goes away, and it's a lifetime of moving forward and learning how to live with emotional pain that is always present. People need to learn that they will lose friends who don't know how to be there for them or that can't accept the fact that you are a different person now. People need to know that they will gain new friendships with deeper connection and meaningful perspective.

Even more important than learning about how hard it is to lose a spouse due to death, I want people to know that through it all, God really does have a purpose for it. God will never waste a hurt. He will never allow you to go through tragedy without beautiful purpose behind it. People need to know that there is a way to respond to tragedy and trials with grace and with hope. You are never alone when going through the battles of life. There are more people than not that understand what you may be going through. It is my hope that you will find that I am one of those people. Most importantly, you are never alone in your battles because God is always with you. There is nothing you can go through in this life that Jesus himself didn't encounter when He walked this earth fully man. While it's true that God is ultimately in control of our lives, He still gives us free will. He does allow us to make choices. One of those choices is how to react when unexpected hardships and tragedy hit our lives. I have chosen God. I have chosen to believe that Jesus is the savior of the world. I have chosen to live my life, as well as I can, from His perspective. I have found that when I view my life through the eyes of God and not my own, I eventually gain a peaceful soul. I chose Him, and I found Him deeply along my walk in June. It is my hope and my prayer that you will choose and find Him too, even if it's in the smallest way. You may pleasantly find yourself in great peace even along your hardest walk as well.

ACKNOWLEDGMENTS

First and foremost, all my love to my two boys, Zane and Xavier. The two of you are my reasons for everything. You have no idea of the impact you both have on me. You have no idea how strong, resilient, and wise beyond your years the both of you are. The two of you are why I have persevered and continued to push forward. It is because of you two that I want to live and thrive, and not just survive. There are no other people on this earth that I love and adore more. I am far from perfect, and I know I make many mistakes, but it is my hope and prayer that as the two of you grow, you will be able to look back over your lives and say that your mom made everything okay.

I have so much gratitude and admiration for my parents, Ron and Milly. Mom and Dad, you have always sacrificed for the well-being of all your children. I certainly would not have endured the last ten years without you. Whatever I need, whenever I need it, you drop everything and attend to me. The genuine love and relationship you have built with my two boys is priceless. I don't think I know two other people who are as selfless as the two of you. My heart is full.

I have such a grateful heart for Pastor Don Poest. Pastor Don, you have walked this journey with me from day one. Your wisdom, realness, and compassion have been, and always will be, a true Godsend to me. I always say the sun rises and sets on you. I know you probably wouldn't like that sentiment because you know that it is only God who the sun rises and sets on. Although I know that to be true, Pastor Don, you come in second. My heartfelt thanks are also extended to Pastor Dan Toot. Pastor Dan, you have the sincerest and most forgiving heart of everyone I know. Your persistent pursuit of me when all I wanted to do was quit and run away is beyond appreciated. You will never fully understand the deep gratitude and respect I hold for you. When no one else seemed to care, you did. Despite my chip-on-my-shoulder attitude, you extended grace with no judgement or condemnation. You are a shining example of Christ, who pursues His flock with love when they have gone astray.

I must thank my sister, Re, and two of my dearest friends, Kristin and Paula. All three of you women were my rocks this past year. All of you knew just how to be a friend. You all knew how to just show up and shut up. All three of you so graciously gave up your time when I couldn't be alone. Kristin, you shared your wisdom and advice with me to get me through crisis mode. You called me, listened to me cry, rooted me on and gave me the encouragement that I could get through my intense panic attacks. You always acknowledged my pain and reminded me to never underestimate what I went through. Most importantly, you prayed for me and with me. Paula, you dropped everything, several times, and came right over when I would text you saying I needed you. You spent the night with me, let me cry on your shoulder, and assured me that this was just a bump in my life. You were so certain that in a year I would be a different person. Here I am a year later and you were right. Re, you assured me that there was nothing medically wrong with me. You let me just cry it all out to you. You sent your husband on his way and stayed the night with me for nights in a row because I was so afraid. You gave me the courage to talk to my doctor about medication and reassured me that there was no shame in needing it. You also devoted much time to reading my manuscript and helping me to make changes so that its clarity, sentence structure, etc. could be the best it could be. Your OCD came in handy.

Last, but certainly not least, I must thank my counselor. You are the one who lit a fire under my butt to finish and publish this book. I truly believe that I would not have found Shannon again without your services this past year. You definitely chose the right career and I thank you from the bottom of my heart.

And finally, as always, I acknowledge my Lord and Savior, Jesus Christ, who has written my story and continues to write my story so that I can ultimately tell His story.

CHAPTER 1

How My Walk in June Began

I didn't really want to go camping that weekend in June of 2010. It was two hours away in Pennsylvania. Mark offered to just go by himself with the two boys, and I could stay home if I wanted to. I almost took him up on his offer but decided to just go. I took both boys with me to Zane's karate lesson that Saturday morning while Mark got the camper ready. Zane got started in his class, and I took Xavier and walked down to Starbucks. I talked to my mom about not really wanting to go. But again, I made the decision to just go as I walked back to Zane's karate class. Mark popped his head in toward the end of Zane's class and commented on how stinking cute he looked. He had to get a key that he needed out of the car that I drove, and he then told me he would see me at home.

We got home and started getting everything packed up to go. I was looking after a two-year-old and a five-year-old and packing for me and packing for them. It was chaotic. So I slammed the ketchup and mustard down on the counter when Mark accused me of not helping him get things packed up. We eventually were ready to go. The camper was all hitched up to the SUV, and we were all strapped in and ready to go. Of course, as soon as Mark pulled out of the driveway, I realized I forgot something and ran back into the house. When I came out, Mark had the SUV with the camper in tow, waiting on the street right across from the house. I remember him just sitting in the driver's seat, arm hanging out the window, head turned toward me, face waiting patiently for me to return. It is an image that is etched in my mind. It is indeed the last image I have of Mark leaving our house. Little did I know that this was the last time Mark would be leaving our house—never to return. Thank God, I decided to just go.

We arrived at Virginia's Beach Campground in North Springfield, Pennsylvania, late afternoon on Saturday, June 5, 2010. I don't even know how Mark found this place. It seemed to take forever to get there. It was out in the middle of nowhere. We were supposed to go to a campground near Toledo, Ohio, but Mark canceled that reservation on Friday after he got home from work. A line of severe storms was scheduled to rip through that area. So he found this place instead. Free of storms. That was Mark. Always wanting his family to be safe.

It was a beautiful campground. It butted up against Lake Erie, and there were two rows where campers could set up. We were given a spot up closer to Lake Erie. Mark asked me if I wanted him to go in and change our location to the back row, where there were no other campers set up. I remember saying that being closer to the lake would be nice but staying back would be nice too because we had the whole section to ourselves. There were five or six campers already closer to the lake. I decided on staying back where we had more privacy, so Mark went in and had it changed. Since when did he listen to me?

The boys and I played on the little playground there. Xavier brought cars, and we made roads all over the dirt on that playground. Zane was swinging on the swings and sliding down the slide. There was another little boy and little girl on the playground, and we all talked and played. The boys brought their bikes, so they also rode those. All four of us took a walk around the campground. We walked down to the Lake Erie shore. Rocks were all along the shore—lots of little ones and big ones. We threw rocks into the water to see who could make the biggest splash. Of course, Daddy would pick up the biggest and heaviest ones and make the biggest splashes of all. The boys loved it. I remember Daddy taking a picture of Zane standing on a big rock with Lake Erie behind him. We then made our way to the staircase that led back up to the campsites. We got back to our camper, and Mark got the grill ready. We grilled cheeseburgers and hot dogs. We had corn on the cob and baked beans. We started our fire, and Mark set up the tiki torches around the firepit. We made s'mores. Mark and I had a beer as we watched Zane and Xavier run in the open, grassy area. They laughed and tackled each other. They were wrestling, laughing, and calling each other names. I remember seeing a woman across the way starting her fire and swinging on a swing.

It was getting dark, and the boys were getting tired. I remember telling a Queen Bleuzie story (that was our dog at the time) to the boys as I stood around the fire before I took the boys into the camper to settle down. I got both boys in, and Xavier wanted Daddy. So Daddy of course came in to lie down with Xavier. I fell asleep while lying with Zane. It was only about nine thirty when

Mark woke me up to say that Xavier was asleep. He asked if I was coming out. I told him that I was just going to crash. He said okay and said he was going to have another beer, and then he would be in. Oh, how I wish I could reverse time and sit outside with him and have one last beer. I had no idea that my nightmare would really begin when I woke up about four hours later.

We had a full-size camper, complete with a kitchen, bathroom, and shower, and pop-out beds. I lay on one side of the camper in the pop-out bed with Zane while Mark lay with Xavier on the other side. I woke up around one thirty in the morning to the most horrendous storm that I have ever witnessed. The thunder and lightning were relentless. The pounding rain hitting the canvas above me surely had to be hail. It was scary. In fact, it was so scary that I prayed to God right then and there to keep us safe and protect us through this storm because it was so bad. I said numerous times later that God blew off my prayer.

I woke up and saw that Mark was awake too. We looked at each other with concern because the storm was insane. He then suggested that we move the boys and us to the middle of the camper until this storm blew over. We put Zane and Xavier on the cushions that could be transformed into a bed from the table. They were huddled together, lying on their bellies. I lay in the middle by twisting my body around the seat, and Mark pulled the mattress from the bed he was sleeping on and put it on the floor in the middle and lay back down.

At that moment, I heard it. That sound. That freight-train sound without a whistle. Mark and I looked at each other with looks of complete fear. I then lifted the curtain up on the window to peek outside. That's when Mark saw that the outside awning was still up on the camper. He immediately got up and went outside to bring it down. I remember thinking, *Well, don't go out there!* He wouldn't have listened to me if I said anything. About thirty seconds later, I followed Mark outside. The boys were still snuggled together and quiet. I stood on the outside step of the camper, which was below the camper door. I looked down to my right and saw Mark standing next to the camper, with his arm working fast to bring down that side of the awning. Constant thunder and flashes of lightning *never* stopped.

The next thing I remember is the wind ferociously whipping my hair around my face. I felt the camper hover upward. I took my eyes off Mark and looked up at the camper hovering and thought to myself, *This thing is going to flip over in my direction.* My mind instantly went to the boys, and before I knew it, I was thrown *inside* the camper. I remember my body hitting the counter, hard, and a watermelon exploding around me. Bruises on my forearms and inner thigh the size of baseballs and as dark as midnight were revealed later.

The camper door closed on my foot, trapping it. I was then sitting on the floor with my foot not only trapped in the door but now with it under the door. Suddenly it was completely silent. No thunder, no pounding rain, no lightning. No crashing sounds of a flipping camper.

The only sound now was the screaming of the boys. They were yelling "I want to go home! I want Daddy!" I was screaming "My foot! My foot! My foot!" Little did I know that Mark had just endured something far worse than a crushed foot. I tried to reach for the boys, but I was stuck. I tried to pull my foot out, but it wouldn't budge. I continued to reach for the boys. They continued to scream. They were okay. They fell against the softness of the cushions that you would sit up against while at the table. I told them that I could not get them. They would have to walk over to me because my foot was trapped and could not move. They needed to just take a couple of steps. Zane finally did, but little Xavier was shaking so badly that he couldn't. I just stretched as far as I could, and I pulled him to me. I remember that I kept trying to pull my foot out. I finally gave up. It was not coming out. The boys and I huddled together, screaming, "Daddy! Anybody! *Help! Help us!*"

We sat there, staring up at the toilet that was now on the ceiling. I heard a car start up and was convinced that it was Mark. He must have had the keys, and he was going to get help. We found our flashlight, and I had Zane open the drawers to see if we could find a knife to cut the canvas of the pop-up bed section. I thought if we could cut it, I could send Zane out to run to the main house. We couldn't find it. We continued to scream for help.

My foot at this point was in extreme pain. I looked down at it, and it was obvious it was in trauma. I thought that my foot would not be able to be saved. I don't really know how long we were sitting there. But I was sure that Mark would be back soon with help because I heard him get in the car and leave.

We finally heard a man's voice yelling in to us, "Ma'am, are you okay?" I told him no. "My foot is trapped, and I can't move." He then told me that he was cutting the canvas open. As soon as he opened it, there was another man and a woman who immediately opened her arms for my boys. I told the boys it was okay. "Go with this nice lady." They did. She scooped them both up in her arms.

The two men lifted the camper enough so that I could get my foot out. I pulled it out and then asked the man if my husband was out there. His words: "Ma'am there is nobody out here." I told him okay, because I heard him start the car. He went to get help. He and another man then carried me across the way to his camper because I could not walk. I remember feeling embarrassed because all I had on was a short t-shirt.

They lifted me into their camper, and that's when I met Gretchen. I immediately knew she was the woman who I had noticed swinging earlier when Mark and I were sitting around the fire. She was holding my then two-year-old Xavier in her arms. Zane was walking around her camper exploring it, like he always did when he was somewhere new. He loved that they had a dog with them. She had two kids as well—a boy and a girl. I recognized them as the two other little kids that were playing on the playground the night before.

She then took care of me. I learned that she was from North Olmsted, Ohio, which is only a half hour away from where I lived. She was a former EMT or a nurse, so she was excellent at caring for my foot. She wrapped my foot and did what she could. She wrapped each one of my boys up with a blanket. I remember her looking at her son asking if she could give Zane his sport blanket and said she would buy him another one. The little boy shook his head yes. (We still have that blanket.)

I was sitting in a position in her camper where I could look out a window that faced where our camper was. I do remember wondering why Mark wasn't coming to check on us. I noticed that the car was back, so I knew he was back from getting help. I then asked Gretchen if she could go and see if she could get my husband. She said sure. So she left. As she was gone, I noticed out the window that the camper was now standing back upright. I noticed our SUV was pulled in differently, so I knew Mark was back.

Then I saw Mark, a big guy with wavy kind of out of control hair, wearing a pale-yellow shirt. *Oh, good,* I thought. *There he is, but why isn't he coming to check on us? Who cares about the camper?*

A little while later Gretchen returned with Xavier's "Bear-Bear," another stuffed animal, and a pair of my pants. We joked about being "pantless," and she wanted me to have mine. She reached over and closed the curtain of the window that I was looking out of. I thought it was odd but didn't make too much out of it. I asked her if she saw my husband. I said he is a big guy with wavy hair. She told me that there were a lot of big guys out there. I said, "Oh, well, okay. I saw him through the window anyway." I recall that I then told her, "Wow. He could have been crushed under the camper!" She just shook her head, and she kind of put her face in her camper bathroom. (I found out later that at this point Gretchen knew, but I sure didn't.)

The ambulance and EMTs showed up. They came to Gretchen's camper, and they did what they needed to do to my leg and to my foot. I remember that I kept asking for them to go find my husband and that I really wanted him to come over here. All they kept saying was, "Well, we need to get you and your pain taken care of." They put a towel on my head and around my face. It was still raining, and they made a joke like they were protecting my head and face from the rain with a little babushka.

They then lifted me onto a stretcher and wheeled me over to the ambulance. I remember asking where my boys were. They told me that the boys were right there, and they would get them in the ambulance with me.

Again, I asked where Mark was. "I really want to see him before you take me in this ambulance." I did think it was strange that they were putting the boys in the ambulance with me. Why didn't Mark take them? I started to really panic as they were lifting me into the ambulance. I demanded to see my husband, but no one would listen to me. I finally asked, "What happened? Where is my husband? What happened to my husband?" The woman that was with me, said; "Ma'am I do not know. I have been with you the whole time."

I heard a man say, "I don't know what they are doing with him." I think at that point I may have known. Or I may have thought that he was just really hurt, and they needed to take him somewhere else to treat his injuries. But why wouldn't they just tell me that?

They strapped Zane in behind me, and he was talking up a storm and excited about being in the back of an ambulance. Xavier was crying and strapped into a little seat to the right of me. I held his little hand as I lay there, on the verge of passing out. I was so light-headed—gasping for air and feeling as if I was out of my body. I remember them asking me if I wanted to be taken to Erie Hospital in Erie Pennsylvania or to Brown Medical Center in Conneaut, Ohio. Don't ask me how I even had enough sense to answer, "Brown." I remember thinking it made sense to head back to Ohio instead of going farther into Pennsylvania.

I don't remember much of the drive except for the one man—an EMT—trying to joke and talk to me. I wanted him to shut up. I am sure he was trying to keep me alert.

When we got to Brown Medical Center, they started to lift me out and panic set in again. The woman noticed and commented that I seemed really panicked again. I kept saying, "I don't know why my husband isn't here."

They wheeled me into the hospital and got me settled in a bed. The nurse's name was Shannon. She kept my boys while they wheeled me away for X-rays on my foot. Miraculously, there were no broken bones. Just nerve damage. They wrapped it and wheeled me back to the room.

My two baby boys were sitting in chairs, and Zane could hardly keep his eyes open. Xavier was wide awake and ready to roll. I asked if a bed could be brought in so that Zane could lie down and go to sleep. They happily did so.

I asked for a phone because I wanted to call my parents. They said that they would call them for me. I can't remember the order of what things were said, but I recall them asking me who my next of kin was. They also somehow knew my maiden name was Sutherland. They asked if my parents' number was unlisted because they were having some difficulty finding it. I remember thinking that if they would just bring me to a phone, I would call myself. They came back in a little bit to let me know that they did get a hold of my parents and that they would be here in a couple of hours.

It was probably around three in the morning at this point. They took Xavier because he was wide awake, and they wanted to let me sleep. Only I didn't sleep. Zane did. I remember asking for socks because my feet were freezing and I remember waiting for Mark to come through the doors to get us. I got the socks, but Mark never came. I would hear doors open out by the nurse's station, and I would hear men's voices. Every time I was sure it was Mark coming. It never was.

I would ask for assistance to the bathroom. They gave me crutches because I could not walk. They walked with me to the bathroom. I would ask several times if they heard or knew anything about what was going on with my husband. They never knew anything because they told me they had no connection out there (to the campground). I remember telling them that if they did hear anything to please let me know because I couldn't help but think the worst. They said they would, but they never did.

Zane continued to sleep, and I continued to just lie there wondering, "Where is Mark? This is not right." He would be here. So again, I thought that he must have just gotten a lot more hurt than me. His injuries must require treatment that they can't do here. But why wouldn't they just tell me that?

As I was lying there, I started piecing everything together. My mind was a whirlwind of thoughts: *I heard him start the car and go get help. He went to get help so he can't be that hurt. But, wait. He never yelled in to me and the boys before he left to get help. He would have yelled in to tell us he's going to get help or ask if we were okay. He never did that. That was weird. And then he never came over to Gretchen's camper to check on us. I saw him through the window, though. He would care about seeing me and the boys over getting the camper standing upright. He would have kept the boys instead of them riding in the ambulance with me, or he would have ridden with me in the ambulance. He didn't even come see us before they took us away. Gretchen closed that curtain on that window so I couldn't see out. Why would she do that? They put that towel over my head so I wouldn't get wet. Or was it to block my peripheral vision so I couldn't see our camper. That one man made the comment that he didn't know what they were doing with him (Mark). No. Could Mark have been killed? That's just not possible. Could he be dead? Could he have been under the camper when it flipped over? No. No way.*

I prayed at that moment. I remember looking at the clock. It was 4:00 a.m. *Please, God don't take him. Don't take Mark, but I know*

You already did. I lay there for two more hours wondering, praying, rethinking, praying, feeling numb, praying. I never did sleep. Mom and Dad walked through my hospital door about two hours later. It was now six in the morning.

Speaking of my parents, their perspective on all of this is worth mentioning. It's a parent's worst nightmare to be woken up by a phone call in the middle of the night. Your heart pumps, and your brain starts to think the worst. This most certainly was the case when my parents received their phone call around three in the morning. Mom answered the phone. She was told that there was an accident, but that the boys and I were okay. Whoever called explained the accident to her and told her that the boys were totally fine, and I had an injured foot, but we were all okay. She was then told that they were going to need to come get us. Mom at this point couldn't talk. She was stumbling over her words in high pitch and had to pass the phone to my dad. As he took the phone she got up and quickly changed.

Dad was then told the same thing. When he asked about Mark, all he was told was that he wasn't at that facility. After being told where the boys and I were, they headed out. My parents live a couple of hours from Conneaut, so it would be a little while until they got there. As they were driving, my dad kept saying he just had a funny feeling about Mark. He knew something was not right with Mark. My mom would get angry when he would say that and tell him to just shut up. She was sure he must have had more severe injuries and must have needed treatment elsewhere. Besides, she was convinced that God would never be so cruel as to take Mark away from his wife and two very young boys. There were storms across the area that early morning when my parents were driving.

It was so bad at times that my dad had to pull over because it was Impossible for him to see. I believe they had to pull over a few times, which made their arrival time later than normal.

When they reached the Conneaut exit, my parents noticed right away that there were police cars right off the exit. As soon as they pulled off the exit, the police followed them all the way to Brown Medical Center, pulled right in behind them and parked behind them. Mom and dad had pits in their stomachs, and they knew something awful had happened.

As they got out of their car, the police officer asked, "Mr. and Mrs. Sutherland?" Mom and dad said yes. The police officer then asked them to follow him. Mom asked him if this is something bad. He replied, "Well, it's not good."

Mom and dad followed him into a conference-type room where they were then told exactly what had happened at the campground. He told them that Mark was trapped under the camper when it flipped over and didn't make it. Mom was confused. She asked, "What do you mean, Mark didn't make it? This is a cruel and disgusting joke you are playing here." At that moment, the nurse who was taking care of Xavier all night came in carrying him in her arms. I believe at this point other officers and hospital personal were present. My mom grabbed Xavier into her arms, and they were then led to me.

Dad was the first one through the door, followed by my mom, who was holding Xavier. Dad had tears streaming down his cheeks, and I just looked at him. I said, "It (the camper) crushed him didn't it?" He shook his head yes. I think I cried. I can't really remember. Mom sat on the bed with Xavier and hugged me.

Police officers, nurses, and other hospital personnel were

standing in the doorway and in the room. Zane was starting to wake up. He thought it was cool that he had slept all night in a hospital bed. Some man was holding my hand and apologizing to me that no one would answer me when I asked about my husband. He was the one who told everyone not to tell me anything because he knew I wasn't from the area, and he wanted me to have family with me. I told him that I understood but I knew. I did ask him if he was sure because Mark is a really big guy. He told me it was a really big camper. I asked him, "What do I do? How do I get my stuff," and then I remember shaking my head in total disbelief and shouting a sentence that contained words that I'll leave to your imagination. I remember asking mom to take the boys out of the room so that I could answer the questions from the police officers. I remember talking to a hospital clergyman and telling him that I needed to tell my pastor. He took care of that for me.

I remember being discharged and everyone walking out front with me. I remember walking outside to the breeziest of mornings on crutches with a throbbing foot that would not walk. I remember sitting up front with my dad and heading on a two-hour trip home. I remember Shannon, the nurse, crying and hugging me. She gave me a thumbs-up as we drove away. I remember wondering how I came on this camping trip just yesterday morning with Mark, and now I was coming home with my parents and not with him?

My walk in June had just begun. Only it would be the walk of a lifetime that would constantly be evolving through the years. Little did I know that it would be a walk that I couldn't stop even when I so desperately wanted to. It would also be a walk that I couldn't get enough of at times. Sometimes the walk would turn into a run. Sometimes it would be easy-going and peaceful. Other times—a lot of the times—it would be treacherous, hard, painful. It would be a lonely walk often, and sometimes I would have company. Little did I know that this walk would be one that would change the core of who I am. It would test my faith. It would bring me to my knees in tears, anger, pleading, worship, and praise to the King. It would be a walk of twists, turns, and surprises. It would be a walk that I couldn't stop—a forever walk that would shape me into the woman that God intended for me to be.

CHAPTER 2

My Life with Mark

I met Mark Joseph Savage in the summer of 1995. I was twenty-three years old, and he was twenty-one. Yes. I am a cradle robber. I was working at a day care center while I was waiting to get a full-time teaching job. Mark was working next door at a tool rental place where they rented out miniexcavators, bulldozers, and things like that. I would take the kids outside to play on the playground, and that's when I spotted Mark across the fence. I thought he was interested in the girl that I worked with. I did, however, learn he was interested in me when I spotted a note that he had left on the windshield of my car one Friday afternoon. It was his last day of work because he was starting law school at Cleveland Marshal School of Law. He was such a sarcastic and funny man even then with his note to me. It read: "I've been intrigued by your beauty all summer long. If you are interested in doing something this weekend, or any time, give me a call." His number was then scribbled down at the end of the note. Well, of course I was interested, and I laughed at his pick-up line, but I didn't want to seem desperate or too anxious, so

I at least waited until Sunday afternoon. He told me that he really did wait around all weekend for my call. I was even the cause of his breakup with his then current girlfriend. Oops.

Mark kept me out until four o'clock in the morning on our first date. We went to dinner, and then as a spontaneous, in-the-moment decision, we ended up in the flats in downtown Cleveland. That didn't go over too well with my parents, who were both waiting up for me when I walked in the house. I got quite the earful about how I was out all night with some strange guy and how anything could have happened. It was very funny to watch Mark kiss up to my dad when he first officially met him. "Hello, Mr. Sutherland. It is so nice to meet you, Mr. Sutherland."

I knew I was going to marry Mark on our first date. I mean, really. I did. So did he. We talked about that several times later. He told me later after we were established in a relationship that on our first date, he knew I was "the one" when I cried over a stray little dog that looked so sad and lonely, hovered up in the corner of a building. He told me that at that moment he knew I was different and that he was going to marry me, and four years later, he did. We really did know that we were going to get married on that first date, but we weren't crazy or stupid about it. We knew that getting to know each other takes time, and there was so much that both of us wanted to accomplish before marriage. We dated for four years, and we truly did become the best of friends in that time. I did get into a full-time teaching position, and Mark plugged away at law school. We had a lot of fun during those dating years—boats and jet ski weekends on Lake Erie, going out to clubs with friends, minivacations, and lots of learning about each other. It was a fun and carefree time. He finished law school and was established in his first job as a lawyer during our dating time.

Mark asked me to marry him in November of 1998. He was sneaky and romantic. He asked me to go away with him for work. He made it sound like it would be fun if I went with him since neither of us had ever been to Maine. I remember having a big presentation due for my master's program the week after we got back. I almost didn't go because of it, but Mark was so insistent. I did get the presentation done before the weekend, and I went. We flew to Maine, and he played it off that he wanted to see this pretty lighthouse. (We liked lighthouses.) We ended up at the Portland Head Lighthouse in Cape Elizabeth, Maine. It was beautiful. It sat among the rocks right along the rugged Maine coast. We climbed over the fence to stand on the rocks right in the middle of the water, with the lighthouse in the background. It was chilly and breezy with slight waves. That's where he did it. He got down on one knee, told me how much he loved me and asked if I would marry him! I was shocked. I had no idea he was doing that. There was no work-related trip. This trip was all about us getting engaged. I cried, called him a dork, and said yes! We stayed in a very cozy bed and breakfast not far from the lighthouse for the whole weekend. It was a surprise, romantic engagement that blew me away.

We got married on October 23, 1999. It poured on our wedding day. It poured so hard that you could have taken a boat to our wedding. However, the day was perfect. With the rain coming down, and the harpist playing inside my cozy little childhood church, my wonderful groom waiting for me at the end of the aisle, it couldn't have been more perfect. I was cool, calm, and collected when I walked up the aisle. Mark, on the other hand, cried like a baby when he watched me walk up to meet him. He was so sweet. The pastor read out loud what we wrote about each other. I said that Mark was like this best friend that I have known all my life that has finally come home. Mark said I was like his personal lighthouse that guided his way when he got lost. The ceremony concluded, and we had a party of a lifetime afterward. It was the wedding of my dreams filled with family, friends, fun, and, most importantly, the love of my life. It concluded with an awesome two-week honeymoon in Hawaii.

We had a blessed marriage. I finished my master's degree in education during this time. Mark worked his way up to becoming a top-notch attorney at one of the biggest law firms worldwide. We bought our house and continued to have a relationship that was free from stress, drama, and fighting. It was just something we never really did. We were blessed financially. We enjoyed vacations. We became faithful members of our church, where Mark played bass for the worship band. We loved each other and, even better, we liked each other. We took marriage seriously. We took having children seriously. That's probably why it took us five years of marriage before we decided to have children. I recall us, at one point, having two convertibles. We made the comment that we were making the point that we aren't having kids. Two weeks later I found out I was pregnant. Well, bye-bye to two convertibles, but I never did and never will buy a minivan!

Zane, our first child, was born in 2005. He was and still is a blessing. However, that stress-free, no fighting marriage I just talked about? Well, let's just say having babies is a game changer in your marriage. Everyone talks about how great it is to have a baby and how you will love your spouse even more. Um ... what planet are those people living on? No. It was not great having a baby, and for me, it was just the opposite of loving your spouse more. I wanted to kill him! Having a baby is hard work. It's stressful, it's confusing, it's emotional, and it's draining. I suffered from postpartum depression badly and needed the help of medication to get me out of the hole I was in. Mark was not the most supportive husband with this. He just didn't and couldn't understand any of it. He also went through a postpartum depression of his own. We really were on the verge of divorce with him not knowing if he loved me or wanted to stay married to me anymore. I was devastated and at a loss of what to do. I was angry, hurt, and confused. I did seek advice and continued to "stick it out" because I knew we were not done. We ended up just coexisting in the house for a good six to eight months. He did his thing. I did mine. Things did settle down, and we became civil and nice to each other again.

We were asked, out of the blue, to join a marriage group with three other couples. It was a group that was designed to keep marriages strong based on Christian principles. Coincidence that this opportunity presented itself when it did? I think not. I was all for it but didn't know how Mark would be with it. Surprisingly, he said, "Why not?" It wasn't until after we got into this group that we were finally able to open up to each other, cry about what had been going on, really listen to and understand each other, and let go of hurt feelings and emotions. Mark asked why I didn't leave him because any other woman would have. I remember simply telling him, "Because I love you. You are who God has chosen for me to spend my life with. You just don't give up." He then said he would spend the rest of his life making this up to me, and he did. No great marriage is without crisis. Our marriage was no exception. I do believe our marriage was saved and made stronger when we let Christ enter our marriage during that marriage group time.

Xavier, our second son, was born in 2007. We were so thrilled to have another boy. Mark always wanted two Savage boys, and we knew our family was complete. The both of us knew that we were done with having children. We never wanted a third. Life was good. It was more than good. It was amazing. We had a strong marriage once again, two happy and healthy baby boys, two careers that were stable, and we were healthy with healthy extended families. Life was more stressful, and we did seem to have more disagreements than we ever did before. That's what having kids does. I think that's just the reality of life, but overall, we were strong, we were happy, and we were in it for the long haul until we were one hundred years old. Mark was a great husband once again and an amazing daddy to his two little boys, whom he adored and said were his two greatest accomplishments ever! We were on top of the mountain, so to speak. It was so easy for us to praise God because our lives were "perfect." Even though Mark still played bass in the worship band, and I helped in the church nursery from time to time, we did become inconsistent with our church life, but we were still grateful, and we still believed in God. God knew we loved and believed in Him, so of course we believed that He would continue to bless us.

The most significant aspect of our relationship was not our ability to get through tough times. It was not that we were financially secure. It was not that we were "two peas in a pod." It was not even the births of our boys. The most significant aspect of our relationship happened on Christmas Eve, 1995. Let me back up a bit. One of my most treasured memories of our dating life was how often we would go to parks, lay a blanket out under a tree, and talk for hours. Another treasured memory was spending hours drinking coffee and tea at Friendly's restaurant well into the night. We would often close the place down. Those moments are the times we really got to know about each other.

During our many talks, I learned that Mark really did not believe what the Bible said. He claimed to have read it from cover to cover. He thought it was a good guide in how to live your life, but believing it's divine and the true word of God was just something he couldn't buy into. He guessed he believed in Jesus, but he didn't put too much thought into this whole religion thing. Now, I became a true Christian when I was a fifteen-year-old girl. I remember lying in my bed and making the decision to follow Christ. I knew how important it was to be dating someone who had similar beliefs as me. I was bound and determined to teach Mark and show him differently. I was concerned, though. Here I was, knowing full well that I was totally falling in love with Mark, but I was really questioning if I should be dating him. How can I be with someone who doesn't believe the Bible to be the true word of God and doesn't give too much thought into Jesus? I mean, I didn't need a crazy, over the top faith, but I needed the same general belief system.

I continued to date Mark, obviously, and I talked to him about what it really means to be a Christian. I was fearful of looking like I was one of those crazy, religious, holy-roller fanatic people. I was not very bold in my faith back then. However, the foundation of Christ was laid down for me the night I accepted Him. Even back then, He was guiding me and would not let me stray. I shared the scripture of John 3:16 with Mark: "For God so loved the world that he gave his one and only Son, that whoever believes in him shall not perish but have eternal life" (NIV). I shared with him that it was so much more than just saying, "I believe in it." I told him you must say it, aloud, in prayer, to Him, that you accept Him. That you want Him to forgive your sins. That you want Him to be the center of your life. I shared Romans 10:9 with Mark: "If you declare with your mouth, Jesus is Lord, and believe in your heart that God raised him from the dead, you will be saved" (NIV). I remember being so concerned about this whole thing that I wrote Mark a letter explaining how important my faith was. I told him that I was falling in love with him, but I couldn't be with someone who didn't have any faith at all. I knew that it was important for our relationship and for any future children to be somewhat on the same page with this. He didn't need to be fanatical. He didn't need to believe exactly what I believed in. He didn't need to agree on everything but there needed to be a faith in God. He needed to believe that this world is not all that there is. I wanted him to let me know if he ever made the decision to accept Christ and follow him.

So back to Christmas Eve, 1995. It was a bittersweet Christmas Eve. It was the day my grandmother, my dad's mother, died of cancer. With a sad and heavy heart, my family grieved for my grandmother that day. I remember Mark being with me at my parents' house. It was just nice to have him there. Mark was pretty much a staple at my house since we had reached the point in our relationship where we basically saw each other every day. Mark and I had left to go somewhere, and I can still recall exactly where we were on the road when he told me the news that changed his destiny forever. We were just down the road from my parents, between West River Road and Columbia Road. It was dark out; he was driving, and Mark said to me, "You know that letter you wrote me. The one about accepting Jesus. I just want you to know that I did that the other night. I prayed that prayer and did that." What an incredible gift on Christmas Eve! I remember hugging him and feeling beyond the moon. I was 100 percent convinced from the get-go that Mark was who I was meant to spend my life with. Christmas Eve, 1995, was what clinched it completely for me. The love of my life was truly sitting next to me, and things were never better. I can recall several times throughout our relationship and marriage, Mark saying to me that he was forever grateful to me for sharing who Jesus was, and is, with him. He said it was because of me that he made the decision that would ultimately allow him to live forever. I never realized just how important it was for me to share Christ with Mark in our early days of dating until God called him home in 2010. I never really understood the depth of that decision Mark made until he went home to heaven. He thanked me for it, but it was all God. I was simply the tool He used to reach Mark. It should be a lesson to all of us to share the gospel and the love of Christ whenever, wherever, and to whoever, no matter how much someone may think you're a crazy, fanatic religious person.

I have often said that Mark and I got robbed. We got robbed out of a fifty-year marriage. We got robbed out of raising our boys together. We were the real thing, and it's just so unfair. I have come to realize, though, that we didn't get robbed. We were given the time that was enough for us according to God. In my eyes, I don't always think it was enough, but God's plans sure trump mine. What Mark and I had was beautiful. It was real. It was fun. It was ours. What we had is something that others may never get a chance to have. Our marriage was not always easy, and it would have been easy to just quit, walk away from each other, and divorce. We didn't. We stuck it out even when we were so angry at each other and hated each other. We reconciled through the rough times and came out stronger because of it. In marriage vows, it says "until death do us part." Of course, when we say that, we think not until we are old and gray. At least I did. I certainly didn't think that "until death do us part" would happen when Mark was just thirty-six, and I was just thirty-eight. It did though. It blindsided me, but it didn't blindside God. Job 14:5 tells us how God knows the amount of days we will live. "You have decided the length of our lives. You know how many months we will live, and we are not given a minute longer" (NLT).

Mark and I did marriage right. We made it. We did it the right way and were married "until death do us part." I smile at that. I'm proud of that especially because we had a period where we almost did quit. That brings me joy. That brings me peace. My time with Mark on earth may be over, but what a joyous occasion it will be when I meet up with him again. In our "real" home where our relationship will continue, not as husband and wife, but in a much more complete way as brother and sister in Christ, while dwelling with Christ. Until we meet again, God blesses me with His awesome gift of memories. So I will remember our earthly life together and treasure it until we live together again in the heavenly realm. To think it's all possible because Mark made that decision to accept and because I made that decision to share. Those decisions truly became the most significant ones in our lifetime together.

CHAPTER 3

The "What-Ifs" and the "If-Onlys"

Those first few days, weeks, and months after Mark died are indescribable. If there is hell on earth, that time frame was surely it. The whole first year, really, is a blur with certain memories that God chose to be worthy enough to remember. I would not wish the pure agony of those beginning months on my worst enemy. To say that it was surreal and bizarre is an understatement. I would sit out on my front porch, watch the world go by, and wonder why the world hadn't stopped. I screamed inside, "Doesn't everyone know what just happened? My world is over! Why isn't everyone else's over too?" It made no sense. God took me from the highest mountain to the deepest valley of my life that Sunday in June of 2010. The world did not care. I was certain that the rest of my life would be spent in the deepest of pain with no end. I would go through Wendy's drive-through, order Baconator sandwiches, eat them in the parking lot at nine at night, and just watch the cars speeding by. I thought that I would either get skinny or fat over this whole experience. I guess I was choosing fat. What did I care?

My life had changed forever, and I was convinced that it had not changed for the better.

The days were long and filled with every emotion known to man. I could be laughing and then in ten minutes crying. I would believe one minute that I was going to be okay and then in the snap of a finger was feeling defeated and hopeless with the unshaking feeling that I would never survive this. I felt like I was totally insane. I don't remember that summer very much. My mom was around a lot. She told me I was always going somewhere. She said I spent a lot of time with some friends who I've known all my life and are very wise in the Word of God. Mom said I shopped a lot. I called it retail therapy. I don't recall the boys very much either. Mom said she had them most of the time. I remember embracing the night. It would get dark, and I remember thinking, "Oh, good. It's bedtime. Another day down." Another day down to what, I don't know. It was just another day down.

I slept well. It was my escape from my life. It was an escape from the tragedy—the reality that Mark died. I never had an issue with sleeping in those beginning days. I never had any nightmares or listless nights. Nighttime was my comfort. Beautiful sleep that I never wanted to wake up from. The only problem I had with the night was that it was too short. I would wake up in the morning and without wanting to, replay the reality of what had happened. For weeks and for months I replayed every detail of that weekend over and over in my mind like a movie on constant rerun. Morning was by far the worst time of the day. It was a sinking feeling. It was an achievement if I even got out of bed. I was really excelling if I took a shower. Cards and letters were coming in the mail every day. Not just one or two of them here and there. Dozens upon dozens of them. I hated them. I wanted nothing to do with them. Why would people think that I wanted to read, repeatedly, a reminder of the fact that Mark died? I would throw them in a pile that would build so high that I would finally give in to reading them a few months later. Even then, I read them with no emotion. I was completely numb, and I wanted nobody. Not even my boys.

I felt smothered by my mother, and we ended up having to separate for a short time. She always wanted to be there and hug me and cry with me, but I was overwhelmed, smothered, and, honestly, I needed to grieve at times, completely alone. It was a strange concept to feel so separated from my mother. She is my best friend and is whom I treasure the most in my life, but alone is what I wanted and needed. No one, not even my mother could fix things or help me. I now understand that I was never alone, however. God walked with me. God held me. I grieved. With just me and God!

My emotions were everywhere: happy, sad, depressed, and angry! Oh, I was so angry! My anger hit the roof on one summer day when I was in the car. I was out and about doing who knows what, and I remember having to park in a parking lot. I parked in a spot that was completely isolated, and that's when it happened. I screamed. I screamed my head off with the loudest, angriest, most piercing shrills your imagination can think of. I screamed so loud and so long that I'm surprised I didn't break my windows. I was screaming and crying all at once.

I remember hitting my steering wheel. Hitting the dashboard. Whatever I could find to hit in that car, I hit. I bruised the sides of my hands, and my voice went hoarse. I swore at God. Oh, I swore like I've never sworn before. I said every word you can think of. I called out to God in desperation to please, please, please send Mark back down from heaven. If God was truly a God of miracles, surely, He could do that. Just send him back to me. I wanted my Mark. I wanted my Pooh Bear. I didn't want to be here in this life without him. I didn't know what to do. I was stuck. I was lost. I was dead myself. I'm not sure how long I was in that car that afternoon. All I know is that I hated God. I wanted nothing to do with Him. I told Him that he was selfish for taking Mark from us. Mark was mine and God could not have him. God took Mark away without any concern to what it would do to me or to the boys.

Shortly after the accident, all the "what-if" questions and the "if-only" statements set in. What if we had never gone camping? What if I had just put my foot down and said we are not going. Would we have been safe at home? What if I had decided to stay home and let Mark go by himself with the boys? Would the outcome of the accident be different? Perhaps Mark would have never gone outside of the camper. Would his death still have happened, leaving the boys trapped inside all alone, scared and screaming? What if we hadn't gone camping there? What if we were at another campground, free from storms? Would we have woken up, normally, on Sunday morning ready for breakfast?

What if I had said to keep the camper in the original spot that the campground assigned us, up closer to the lake? We were the only thing in that entire campground that was touched by that tornado. Nothing was affected by the eighty-to-one-hundred-mph wind except for our camper, in that exact spot! Would we have been safe in our original, assigned spot? If only I had said to keep it as is. I was the one who made the final decision to move.

If only I had not lifted the curtain on the window to look outside. Mark wouldn't have noticed the awning was up and gone outside. If only I had told him to not go outside. Would he have listened to me and still be with us? What if he hadn't got that awning down? Would we all still be alive or is it possible that the awning could have worked like a sail, in that horrific wind, and sent the whole camper flying, killing us all?

What if Mark hadn't suggested moving the boys to the center of the camper before he went out? Would they have been hurt or killed because they would have been tangled in the canvas pop-out beds with metal poles, instead of falling against the soft cushions?

If only Mark saw the camper falling over before it hit him in the head. Would he have had enough time to get out of the way? If only the camper hit him in the back of the head and not fallen on top of him. Would he still be alive? Would he be living his life as a vegetable?

What if, when the camper hovered up and flipped over, I fell off the step that I was standing on outside the camper door? Instead, I went inside the camper. What if the logical had happened, and I fell out? Would I have been killed underneath the camper too, leaving those two boys alone, with no idea where their parents were?

I know every single detail of that night. All of it. The only thing I did not see was Mark being hit in the head and falling under the camper. When the camper started to hover, my eyes went off Mark, and I looked up at the camper and watched it flip. What if I had seen Mark fall and get trapped underneath? Would I have been completely hysterical and not able to be in enough control to calm the boys? Would I have that image etched in my mind for the rest of my life, taunting me, giving me nightmares, as that would have been my last image of Mark?

What if, if only. What if, if only. So many of them. I obsessed on them for a long time. They drove me crazy. I blamed myself. I thought of all the things I could have said and done that would have prevented this tragedy. I developed survivor's guilt, and I was sure that I was absolutely no use to anybody, especially to Zane and Xavier. I questioned everything. I understood nothing. Nothing made sense, and the more I questioned and wondered why, the more confused and angrier I became. Then, as quickly as I became confused and angry, I also became overwhelmed with Him.

We hear all the time that God works in mysterious ways. The thing is that it really is true. During this time frame, those immediate months that followed the accident, God showed up in full force, exhibiting His power, His strength, His truths. Despite my anger, my turmoil, and my constant what-ifs and if-onlys, God revealed Himself to selfish little me. Despite all my cursing Him, resisting Him, wanting nothing to do with Him, He stayed with me anyway. His big shoulders could handle my anger and my cursing. He let me do it and stayed at my side 100 percent. I think people don't know, or they forget, that we can let go of Him, but it doesn't matter, because He never let's go of us. When we can't cling to Him, He does it for us and clings so tightly to us that we have no choice but to turn around and fall into His arms. That was me. I let go of Him. Or at least I wanted to. But He wouldn't let me. After all, I was fifteen years old when my foundation of Christ was laid down forever. It doesn't ever go away. Ever since that day, He has hung onto me even when I didn't know it. It was during this time that God would reveal truths to me that I had never understood before.

It was an odd thing to hate God so much but love Him with such an intensity all at the same time. It was a confusing thing to want to run as far away from Him as possible but need to immerse myself in Him to the point that I couldn't breathe without Him. I can't really recall how it all began, but He was so prevalent in my life. I was reading through scripture in a way I never did before. Honestly, I never spent any time reading the Bible when Mark was alive. A verse here and there but that was it. No studying the word, no understanding it except for at a very surface level, and certainly never to the point that I couldn't get enough of it.

It was God and me, up on a mountaintop, alone, with no one else, with scripture just popping out at me so fast and so furious that I could hardly keep up. It was as if I was His only priority, and I began to run to Him instead of away from Him. I began to crave Him and what He wanted me to learn and understand. All my what-ifs were starting to diminish slowly but surely. I learned that God doesn't do "what-ifs" and "if-onlys." He doesn't carry out His plan regarding how we do or don't do something, and I came to the realization that this is true when it comes to our earthly death.

Job 14:5 is a verse that knocked me to my knees. "You have decided the length of our lives. You know how many months we will live, and we are not given a minute longer" (NIV). It wouldn't have mattered if we stayed home. It would not have mattered if I didn't give the okay to move our camper to the other site. It would not have mattered if we were at a different campground. The ending of Mark's earthly life was going to be June 6, 2010, no matter what. Psalm 139:16 proves that God is omniscient. He knows *everything*! He knows the number of hairs on our heads. He knows how many stars are in the sky. "You saw me before I was born. Every day of my life was recorded in your book. Every moment was laid out before a single day had passed" (NLT).

He knew when Mark was going to be born. He knew when

Mark was going to meet me. He knew on our wedding day that our marriage would come to an end by death do us part, only after a short ten years, and He certainly knew that Mark would be coming home to heaven on June 6, 2010. We are all given an appointed time to die from God, and nothing can be done to stop it. Hebrews 9:27–28 tells us: "Just as people are destined to die once, and after that to face judgement, so Christ was sacrificed once to take away the sins of many, and he will appear a second time, not to bear sin, but to bring salvation to those who are waiting for him"(NIV).

Mark could not have escaped his earthly death no matter how things may have been done differently. I realized that no matter how much I played the "what-if and if-only game," the outcome would always be the same. Nothing that I could have done would have changed what God already knew would happen. Mark's death didn't, and nothing ever does, blindside God. Unfortunately, things blindside us, but if we have a Christ-filled heart, He will bring us to the point of being past blindsided—to complete comfort and peace, knowing that things have gone according to His will and for a bigger purpose.

"So, Christ was sacrificed once to take away the sins of many" (Hebrews 9:28 NIV) brought on a huge "ah-ha" moment for me. All my what-if questions led to an ultimate what-if question one day. What if Jesus had refused to go to the cross? What if He simply said no to the Father? Jesus, being fully man, must have felt an incredible amount of fear, anger, and frustration. I am sure He wanted to just scream no and run. Then Jesus, being fully divine, wanted nothing more than to be obedient to His father.

Put yourself there, in his place, if you can even fathom it. There He was, in the Garden of Gethsemane, praying for His Father to take this burden from Him: "Abba Father, he cried out, everything is possible for you. Please take this cup of suffering from me. Yet I want your will to be done, not mine" (Mark 14:36 NLT). I get it! This resonated with me. Not that I can, or you can, totally identify with Christ, but I felt those exact words.

I pleaded for God to just send Mark back! God can do the impossible, so I wanted Him to do so, and send Mark, floating on a cloud, back to earth and drop him right off at my house, but what I was starting to realize was that I did want God's will for my life. I was starting to see that His ways are ultimately better, even if from a human perspective His ways didn't appear to be so. So it hit me like a ton of bricks.

Jesus prayed out, calling for His father to take this horrible burden from Him. He didn't want to endure it, but He knew it was far better to follow His father's will than His own. He knew that being obedient to the Father served a greater purpose than the pain of the "here and now." So He endured the cross. He endured the physical agony of the beatings He received. He endured the crown of thorns pushed into His head. He endured the nails piercing His hands and feet that held His body to the cross. He endured the unthinkable emotional distress of the sins of the world on His shoulders, as He felt abandoned by the Father.

Look what He did? Look what He did for me? Where would I be today if He had not died on that cross? Where would Mark be right now if He had not died on that cross? Where would any of us be if He had not died on that cross? I get it! I get it! My emotional wound left by the loss of Mark is great, but His wounds were greater, and look what happened because He endured what His father asked Him to endure? The sacrifice of His life defeated death. His sacrifice saves us from being separated from God. His sacrifice secures our eternal life with Him, forever, when our earthly life is up. His sacrifice rescues us and enables us to fully live in a way that is far greater than living on earth could ever be. His sacrifice is a gift for those of us who choose it. His tragedy, of having to die on the cross, served the greatest purpose of the bigger picture, and although my tragedy will not take on the sins of the world, it will indeed be used for a greater purpose. It will be used to help others in similar need, and it will be used to bring others to Him.

I realize that I am to share the story that was written out for me by God, to share the news of Jesus Christ. God did not take Mark to just take him and leave me in pain for the rest of my life. He took Him safely home to heaven, so that I could share all that He revealed to me during this tragedy, so others can hear the truth of the gospel. The greatest comfort in sharing my story is knowing that Jesus gets it when I say I want to give up. He understands when I say I don't want to endure the will of God. He didn't want to either that night in the Garden of Gethsemane. His fully human attributes allow Him to identify with me. He will hold me up by His strength when my humanness fails me. He will get me through it to see the bigger picture, because He himself did what was asked of Him for the *big* picture. If Jesus did it, so can I, only because He dwells within me. I would not be able to persevere any other way. He is bigger, stronger, and more powerful than any other force that tries to overwhelm my soul. My soul belongs to Him; therefore, He will carry me through to completion.

CHAPTER 4

The Day I Hated Shopping

I had to tell Zane that his dad died. I had to say those exact words. Later that Sunday, after I arrived home with my parents, Zane was asking about Daddy. Did Daddy get really hurt? When will he be coming home? He even thought Daddy beat us home because his car was in the garage when we arrived. After talking with my pastor, I knew I had to tell him that his father is dead and never coming back. I had to be careful with my words. I didn't want to say things like, "he went to sleep," because to a five-year-old child, when you go to sleep, you wake up. Daddy was not going to wake up, and he needed to know that.

I remember my house being full of family and friends that day. People just kept coming by. I needed to talk with just Zane, and I couldn't find anywhere private and quiet to do so. So I took him on a walk down the street. My sister Re came with us. We walked down the sidewalk, and we sat under a tree. I explained that Daddy got really hurt under the camper. I explained that sometimes people's bodies get so hurt that they can't get better or be fixed, and that is what happened to Daddy. I knew I needed to say the words, and it had to have been all God who gave me the strength to say it, because to tell your child that his or her father died is something that is humanly impossible to do with your own power. So I told Zane that since Daddy's body got so hurt that it can't be fixed, he died. I remember Zane looked at me with his mouth wide open, and he said, "Daddy really died?" I had to tell him yes. I had to tell him that he is not able to come back. I had to tell him that we won't be able to see him again. I had to explain to him that it will be okay, because Jesus took him to heaven where he gets to live with Him, but since he gets to live in heaven now, he can't live here with us anymore.

I had to explain that this is why there are so many people at our house today. I had to explain that people are sad and crying because they love Daddy, and they are going to miss him. I remember telling him that even though Daddy is in heaven now, it's still okay to feel sad. It's okay to cry if you feel like it. Zane just kept saying, "I can't believe Daddy actually died." Then he would talk about some random topic just like any typical five-year-old child. We walked back to the house, and as we approached the driveway, Zane noticed Mark's car in the garage and said, "Well, since Daddy died and isn't coming back, can I have his car?" That comment did make me laugh.

I never had a "Daddy died" discussion with Xavier. He was only two. He was a baby. Xavier just grew up with a life without his dad. It is something he doesn't know any differently. Later that night, when the three of us all slept in my bed, that first night without Mark, Zane cried and said, "I wish we had never gone camping." I simply said, "Me too. Me too." Xavier snuggled in, with a little sad face that showed he just somehow knew life had changed drastically. Even though he was only two, he knew. We huddled together, and I just dreaded the next day because the next day would be the day that I planned the unthinkable—my husband's funeral.

Funeral homes smell. They just do. The funeral home that took care of Mark was certainly no exception. When I walked in, I was just overwhelmed with death. Why didn't it smell of sugar cookies or of cinnamon apples? It was this stale, almost moldy smell that only strengthened the nausea that was already full in my stomach. My sister went with me.

I paused outside the doors, took a deep breath and entered. My dad, my good friend Lisa, and Mark's brother and sister were already there. We sat in a room around a large table with one of the funeral directors. There were so many details to go over, and, honestly, I can't remember how it all went. I do remember being so thankful that I had trusted souls with me. They were able to handle things when I just couldn't. They were able to remember things that I couldn't. Lisa wrote the obituary for the newspapers. My dad reminded us all of Mark's Angel Flight charity, and that donations could be made instead of sending flowers. I mean seriously, who wants flowers?

It's funny how my mind wasn't completely sound but when asked what I wanted printed on the "In Memory" cards, I knew right away that I wanted Philippians 1:3: "I thank my God every time I remember you"(NIV). That has *always* been a favorite verse of mine. God was at work within me, even when I didn't know it.

I love to shop. I love to shop for clothes, home décor, shoes, books, food, anything and everything. However, "shopping" for my husband's casket took shopping to a whole new level. I walked around the "showroom" of sample caskets and looked through catalogs—dozens of them. All different styles, with different colors and different prices. Oh, the prices! Some of those things go for $20,000!

It was the most surreal and ridiculous shopping trip of my life. I remember even saying out loud, "Wow. I really love shopping, but this is ridiculous." I had to pick a color. I had to choose the inside casket lining. I had to even order one that was "XL" because of the size of my husband. Did you ever think there was such a thing as an extra-large casket? So I picked one. I do remember talking out loud and talking through what Mark would or would not like. He would not have wanted me to spend a lot of money on a stupid casket. So I was careful to pick one out that was pretty but cheap, or at least cheaper. Are caskets pretty? Anyway, I thought, *Well, he likes that dark cherry wood color, and he would want the inside to be puffy because he would want to be snuggly in there.*

Then the discussion about the cement vault and the vault liners came into play. They had choices of liners that ranged from extra thick and extra strong that kept all moisture from reaching the casket to preserve the body, to the bare minimum of protection. They even had samples to show me how this all worked, and that's when I lost it. I got up and had to leave.

I left the room, and I collapsed on a couch out in the hallway. I remember sobbing—gut-wrenching sobs. Uncontrollable sobs. I was screaming inside: *What am I doing? How is this happening?* My bear's body is going to be put into the ground never to return. His body is going to go in a big wooden box, and I can't go with him? I just kept thinking: *His body is going into the ground. His body is going into the ground. His body is going into the ground!*

My sister sat with me. Crying with me. I was so hot. I felt sweat pour out of me everywhere. I was light-headed. I could feel myself on the verge of passing out. I couldn't breathe. I had to get out of there. Somehow my sister managed to walk me outside where I sat on the sidewalk, just gulping down air and dry-heaving as I did so. I never totally passed out. I sat for a long while and regained composure. I sat facing the Wendy's that was across the street and realized that I was starving. This was Monday afternoon, and I had not eaten since Mark and I had dinner that Saturday night before we went to bed at the campground. My sister got me water and eventually I went back in to finish the details of the end of Mark's life, and what I thought was the end of mine too.

I was instructed to drop off, or have someone drop off, what I wanted Mark to be dressed in. I remember asking, "Do I send underwear?" It sounds so silly, but do you dress a dead person in underwear? Apparently so, because they said yes. I remember thinking how much Mark hated wearing suits and ties. I almost sent in casual clothes but then I thought it might look inappropriate. After all, Mark was a first-class act, and he needed to look it in his last showing. So I had him dressed in his best suit and tie. However, since the lower half of his body was covered up, I had him buried in his flip-flops because he always wore flip-flops.

I was told later that I handled myself like a boss on that day at the funeral home. I was told that I was sensible, quick to make decisions, knew exactly what Mark would have wanted and not wanted, was level-headed and all around in charge and in control. I guess I take that as a compliment. Is it a compliment that I had handled my husband's funeral arrangements like a boss? I don't know. But what I do know is that if all of that is true—about how I handled myself during that planning—then it surely wasn't me. All credit must go to the overtaking of my human body and human thoughts by the Holy Spirit, because power like that is not humanly possible.

My shopping adventure continued that day, as I went from the funeral home to the cemetery. The cemetery is in Valley City, Ohio, just five minutes from my parents' house. It's a beautiful cemetery, really. It's in the country, and it's not overcrowded. Is that an appropriate word to use? I don't know, but I liked that it was quiet. It was away from hustle and bustle; it wasn't in the center of things. Private, I guess.

I can't even begin to tell you the discussions I had with the man in his office. I have no recollection of what was discussed. My dad was with me, and basically the only thing I remember is that we drove with the cemetery owner around the cemetery looking for a spot. He told me to just take my time and let him know if anything stood out. I picked a spot that was toward the back, away from the road, away from any noise, that was under a tree. Behind the plot is a field, so there is a lot of quietness and privacy. I remember thinking that Mark would like this spot. It's out of the way, far from noise, and peaceful. I ended up buying the plot next to Mark's, and then the two in front. I guess, I felt the need to be prepared and secure our family of four, even if it had to be in burial only. I don't remember much about being at the cemetery that day.

It would be a year and a half later when I would finally revisit the cemetery for the first time. It took me a whole year to design and order Mark's headstone. I just couldn't do it. And even when it finally got done, I still wasn't the one who did it. Two good friends, who happened to be coworkers, did it for me. They were the messengers between the cemetery owner and me. They would go to the cemetery; they would pass on ideas and designs back and forth until the most beautiful headstone was designed. They stepped up and completed one of the most difficult tasks for me, simply because I just couldn't.

CHAPTER 5

Seas of People and the Celebration of Life

The day of the wake came, and I struggled with whether to take Zane. Zane was five. Did he need to see his father laid out? Would it be something that would traumatize him or not even phase him? He knew his dad was dead, but would he try to wake him up? I didn't want to make the wrong decision. I must have changed my mind a dozen times that morning. I was convinced that I was not taking him after he threw up first thing in the morning. I don't know if that was due to a nervous stomach or simply because he had been eating nothing but junk the whole day before because no one was really watching him. It upset me so much that he threw up, and I was determined to protect him, so I decided against taking him.

There was never any question to take Xavier. He was only two. He was a baby and had no clue what was really going on. Plus, I was almost certain that he would have seen Mark lying there, and he would have wanted to crawl on him, snuggle up, and play with Daddy. Nope. I was for sure not taking Xavier.

I was almost ready to leave for the funeral home and something came over me, overwhelmingly, that told me, "Take Zane." That would have made it a dozen and one times that I changed my mind. I took him. Calling hours were from four to eight. I wanted to be there at three so I could go to Mark in private, by myself. I wanted to be able to scream, cry, go hysterical, or do whatever I needed to do in private. Zane stayed outside the funeral home doors with my sister and brother-in-law while I went in with my parents first. There was that disgusting, stale, moldy smell again that hit me as soon as I walked in.

Veronica, the funeral director, was there. She directed me to the room where Mark was laid out. I walked slowly toward the room with my parents and Veronica behind me. I stopped when I reached the room. I was frozen with fear. I had to peek in around the wall. I couldn't fully walk in. When I peeked around the wall, I caught just a glimpse of Mark lying in the casket. That's when I ran. I ran straight to him. I couldn't get to him fast enough. I fell in front of him. I cried. I screamed out loud to him, "I am so sorry this happened to you. I am so sorry. Please, don't go. Don't leave me. I don't want to be here without you." I touched him. His face, his hair, his chest, his hands. I kept sliding my hands into his. He was so cold. Why are you so cold? I kissed him a billion times. My parents stood behind me sobbing. Veronica was off to the side, watching, to make sure things were "okay," I suppose.

I remember sending in a bunch of pictures that I wanted to set up around the casket and inside the casket. I panicked because I did not see them. When I asked Veronica where they were, she showed me where they were, and I moved them. I intended for those to be *in* the casket with Mark. I wanted them to be buried with Mark. I set them all around the inside of the casket. I remember my mom at one point telling me that was enough. I screamed at her, *"No"* and I continued to set them up how I wanted them to be. I continued to touch Mark, to kiss Mark, and to talk to Mark. I told him that I brought little bear (Zane) and that I hoped he was okay with that. I started to calm down, and I got myself together.

It was now time to bring in Zane. I walked out to get him. Zane didn't want to get too close. He wanted to stay back a bit and sit in the chairs. We talked about how it was daddy's body lying there, but his soul, the most important part of who we are, is not there. It is with Jesus, so Daddy cannot wake up or even move. Zane was interested in a candle that was by Daddy's casket and wanted to see the candle close. When I took him closer to look at the candle, he would act like he was interested, but his little eyes kept going down to look at Daddy. He never wanted to stand by the casket. I had to hold him. He didn't want to touch or get too close and that was okay.

He then became interested in everything else at the funeral home. So I walked with him for a bit, exploring the musty-smelling funeral home; that gave my family members and Mark's family members time to see Mark before everyone else started arriving. It was truly amazing how having my five-year-old boy there gave me strength and courage to be there. God knew we needed to be together for that short time. After about an hour, my parents took Zane home to the babysitter, who was already there with Xavier. Mom and Dad then returned, and the calling hours began. It was supposed to be from only 4:00 until 8:00 p.m., but it ended up going well past midnight!

I stood there watching the ever-growing line of people approach me. I wondered why everyone had somber looks. Looks of sorrow and looks of pity for me. I hated it. I wanted to crawl away. I couldn't understand why people were looking at me like that, and then it dawned on me. *Um … Mark died? He's there in the casket just to the right of you?* I still hated it. I can't stand to be a victim. I can't stand for anyone to look at me with pity in their eyes. It came with the territory, I guess. I also remember thinking, *Why am I doing this important event, and Mark isn't standing next to me to greet all these people?* After all, there were so many people I had never seen before. They were connected to him somehow. *Oh, yeah, that's right, Mark died!*

The night carried on. Hundreds upon hundreds of people were coming through the line. I was told that the line got so out of control that it wrapped all the way around the outside of the building, down the street, all the way to the Home Depot. People were standing in line for three hours to get to me and to see Mark. Later, I counted how many people signed the guest book. There were over one thousand signatures. There were my family and friends, my fellow teachers, my church family; high school acquaintances who I had not seen in years came through the line. Former students of mine and their parents paid respect. Mark's family, his coworkers, his friends from all walks of his life made an appearance—his high school buddies, college buddies, law school buddies, fellow attorneys, his boss, his clients, and other professionals from his attorney world. There were so many people that I did not know. How did my husband know all these people? So many kinds of people. The most amazing thing was that all these people who knew Mark came through and told me story after story of what Mark did for them. It was overwhelming really, to find out that my husband was so well loved and so respected. I always knew that, but the stories. The amazing stories of how Mark put himself aside to help so many others, to give others credit, to praise others, and to advance others. I beamed with pride. It was truly a humbling and joyful experience. Mark used to say that he felt as if he never made a difference in people's lives. He often said all he did was save companies millions of dollars—big deal. I certainly pray that he now sees and knows just what an impact he had on people through the little things and through the unselfishness that was Mark Savage. May we learn from this that it doesn't matter what you do in life as a career, but it's how you handle yourself in the career and in life.

One of the biggest highlights of that evening was when I looked out and suddenly, out of the massive sea of people that covered the room everywhere, a group of people emerged. It took me a second to recognize, but it was a big group of Kappa sisters and Heidelberg College friends. Some of these people I had not seen in forever, and I was so overwhelmed with a grateful heart. I remember stepping away from the casket and pulling them through the crowded line to embrace them. Seeing them just did something awesome for my soul. My mom even said that my spirit soared. We talked, cried, and hugged, and as I continued to welcome people, my heart soared with the number of people that loved Mark, loved me, and loved my boys. I remember looking out across the funeral home room, and you couldn't even see an empty space.

So many people mingled and looked at the pictures on the

trifold posters that I somehow put together the day before. People were flipping through photo albums and watching the videos that were so graciously and beautifully put together by two church friends the day before. People were laughing and crying, telling stories.

My mom and Re (my sister) stood with me the whole time, and as people would come through the line, they would tell us how we have at least a couple more hours of people out there. It was amazing that one person was loved so much. It was so beautiful and crushing at the same time. What a legacy. What a testimony. It was well past midnight when the last person made it through the line. I collapsed on a couch, with my head on my brother-in-law's shoulder.

Pastor Don stayed the entire night, and I remember looking at him and saying that I am so proud to be Mark Savage's wife. He told me it was also a testament to who I am as well. I didn't know about that. All I knew was that I just stood at the side of my husband's casket for eight hours, greeting people that loved and adored him. I hugged people, cried with people, laughed with people and heard stories about Mark that I had never known. I was blessed, and I was tired!

I remember Pastor Don telling us all to go home and get some sleep because tomorrow morning would be here fast and Mark's celebration of life service would be upon us. I don't remember going home. I don't remember going to bed, but mom assured me that I sawed logs heavily that night.

My church parking lot was a slew of cars the next morning. I walked in through the doors of my church, with a Bible in hand, to be first greeted by Pastor Don. I remember his hug and his words in my ear: "We are going to carry each other through this." Mark was laid out for viewing in the fellowship area for about an hour before the service started. Again, a sea of people hugging me, crying, offering words of love and sympathy that pretty much went unheard.

People were already seated in the sanctuary, watching the video of Mark that was playing at the funeral home the night before. I could hear the James Taylor music that was set with the video. James Taylor was one of our favorite artists to listen to.

I remember a man introducing himself as Troy, and he told me that he was at the campground. He was there when chaos erupted. He told me how he had read the articles about Mark, and he assured me that Mark may have flown a plane on earth, but he had no doubt that he is flying with the angels now. He told me he just had to come and be here at Mark's funeral today. I was overwhelmed with the kindness of his gesture. I have not been in contact with this man since but would love to see him again one day.

From what I have learned, it was his son that first spotted Mark's feet sticking out from under the camper. This man had called the campground several times to check on any news about me within that first year of losing Mark. I was told it devastated him, as it did a lot of people that were there that weekend. I remember feeling blessed that a man who didn't know us at all, and was from Pennsylvania, came all the way to Brunswick, Ohio, to pay respects to Mark and to us. That is a beautiful memory of that day that will remain in my mind forever.

The time came to close the casket. I leaned over Mark, kissed him one last time, and promised that his boys will always, always know who he is. I promised him that I would carry on, be strong, and make everything okay for the boys. I told him that I am overjoyed to know that he is *home* with Jesus. I kissed him again, touched his hair and his face, and slid my hands into his hands one last time. Pastor Don stood next to me and hugged me close. I told Mark that I loved him and that I will see him on the other side.

Pastor Don helped me along. I walked into the packed sanctuary with my parents and took my seat up front and center. Soon Mark's casket was rolled up the aisle with his closest friends and relatives. It stopped right in front of me, and his beautiful face appeared on the screen. I just shook my head in complete disbelief. All I was thinking was, *How in the world is this really happening?* This accident, this tragedy, this situation is one you hear on the news. These are circumstances that happen to other people, and you mutter how sad and tragic. This doesn't happen to my life. But this was my life. This funeral happening right now was for *my husband,* and I was left behind as the grieving widow with two little boys. Widow. Ugliest word in the world.

The service started with awesome music. Since Mark played the bass in the church worship band, his friend played Mark's bass at his service. The other members and singers that played with him were also up on the altar this day, singing and playing for Mark. I loved it. It was not your solemn, ordinary funeral music, but Mark was not a solemn and ordinary person. Somehow, I got up to speak at my husband's funeral. I don't know how I did it, and I can't remember a lot of what I said.

I remember standing behind the podium, looking out at the array of people. Not one seat was empty. In fact, people were standing up against the walls. I remember blowing the worship band a kiss and telling them that they were awesome.

For whatever reason, God led me to share how Mark had accepted Christ. God also led me to read Psalm 116:15–16 (NLT): "The Lord cares deeply when his loved ones die. O, Lord, I am your servant, born into your household: you have freed me from my chains."

Again, I can't remember all that I said and all that I shared. I was told later that I spoke so well that they wondered how I had time to rehearse. Well, I didn't rehearse what I said. I just stepped up there, and the words came out as is. Basically, I was winging it, which tells me that it wasn't me speaking. It was the Holy Spirit, using my voice as a vessel to say and share what He ultimately wanted me to share. I have a DVD of the funeral. One of these days, I will have to watch it. I have not done so yet.

Everyone was encouraged to come forward and share stories of Mark. So many people did. There were funny stories, stories of success, stories of how he helped others, stories of him growing up. So many different people with so many unique memories of what they did with Mark. It appeared that Mark had connected with people his whole life, and he stayed in contact with people throughout his life. Even though the memories and stories differed, the underlying character of who Mark was stayed consistent. His kindness, his humility, his sense of humor, passion for success, and love of life shone through the stories. It was truly a celebration of Mark's life, and, again, I could not be prouder that this man chose me for his wife.

The service concluded, and the burial took place. I have a very faint recollection of being in a limo, driving to the cemetery, and being at this graveside. Truly, it's a blur. I just remember, once again, too many people to count, too many people watching me with sorrow in their eyes and me feeling too numb to even really feel anything at all. I do remember finally having enough and just leaving to sit in the limo. I watched out the window, at the massive numbers of people laying flowers across his casket that had yet to be put into the ground. We finally drove away, and I just stared out the window, my eyes focused on the casket, hovering above the opening in the ground that it would eventually be lowered into.

We returned to church; my church family had prepared a huge meal. I finally ate. I was *starving*! Whether it was the right choice or not, I had decided to not have the boys at the church for the service. I wanted to protect them, and that is what I decided to do. My parents picked them up and brought them up to the church for the lunch. We stayed for a while; I talked with and visited with people. Again, I have no idea what was talked about and who I even talked to.

I don't remember going home that day, and I can't even begin to tell you what I did over the next few weeks. I do remember having to take Zane to Safety Town the next week. When I was pulling out of the parking lot one day, I saw a friend, more like an acquaintance really, parked next to me. My eyes met hers for a minute and I remember her making a "boo-boo" face at me. Really? A "boo-boo" face? My husband dies, and that's your way of acknowledging me and showing me sympathy? I was disgusted by it. I remember looking at her with a blank stare and then rolling my eyes. I just looked away, pulled out of the parking spot and didn't really even acknowledge her. I don't know why that stands out in my mind. I think it was the beginning of my angry and "you have no clue" mentality that would set in. I think it was the beginning of my doubts about God really caring when His loved ones die like Psalm 116: 15–16 claims. It was the beginning of the longest journey of my life. One that continues today. However, the journey today, compared to the one I was on in those first couple of years after Mark died, is one that has evolved into ultimate trust and faith in Christ.

CHAPTER 6

Healing on God's Timeline

I have learned that it's God's timeline for my healing process. It is God who continuously guides me when milestones need to be attained. There is no rushing, and there are no rules in how one grieves, in how one deals, and in how and when a person conquers painful moments and events. It sounds strange to say that there are times when I have enjoyed the healing process. Yes. I know. How does one enjoy this? Perhaps *enjoy* is not the correct word. I think it's just that I have learned to never, ever let anyone tell me when or how I need to do something. When huge milestones have been conquered, they have been done with such peace and with such clarity that it truly has been God the whole time leading me. I have learned to not listen to anyone, not even myself, but to listen to God only when it comes to accomplishing painful milestones. It was His guidance throughout the whole planning of Mark's funeral that led me to final decisions. I didn't do any of it. He did it all. He continued to guide me and show me when the time was right to conquer things, and once they are conquered, I obtain a sense of freedom, a sense of accomplishment, a sense of greater peace that is not of this world. I walk away from it with healing. A true healing because it was led strictly by God.

One of the hardest things for me to do was to go to the cemetery. I said earlier that I couldn't even get the headstone designed and ordered. I didn't revisit the cemetery until a year and four months later. I decided it was time to go on my anniversary. I just kept hearing God tell me that it was the day to go. So on October 23, 2011, I went to sit before Mark's headstone. I took a Pooh Bear and a Tigger. (After all, I called him bear and he called me tiger.) I also took him his favorite chai tea from Starbucks and an unsweetened tea for me. As I was driving, I was very slow and nervous as I approached the cemetery.

When I entered the cemetery, I had a hard time locating the stone because I couldn't remember being there. Once I spotted the stone in the distance, I froze with fear. It was that same feeling I had when I first walked into the funeral home and froze with fear outside the room where Mark was laid out. As I got closer to the stone, and I could actually read his name on it, it was the same feeling I had in the funeral home when I peeked my head around the corner and caught a glimpse of Mark lying in the casket. I ran to him. I couldn't get there fast enough.

This was the same feeling. I saw his name, and I could not get the car over there and get out of the car fast enough. I was racing to it. I ran to the stone and fell to my knees, in tears! It was so strange to see our names engraved—his name with a final date, but mine not yet complete. I repeatedly traced the letters of his name with my finger.

As I sat there, it was the most bizarre and confusing state of being alive because I had two sets of emotions in sync with each other. One was the most unbelievable, deep, embedded pain that literally took my breath away. It was such pain that my soul just felt as if it was ripped away from me. Yet, at the same time I also felt an overwhelming sense of joy, blessing, and rejoicing knowing that Mark is home, free, at peace, with no stress and in the place I long to be. I was almost jealous of him. I thought about how his earthly body was literally under me and that I was sitting where my earthly body will one day be buried too. Is it gross that I wanted to just sleep there? Is it morbid to say that I wanted to even start digging? I could have stayed longer, but I was starting to freeze. I stayed for about an hour and a half.

As I walked away, I just kept looking back. It was so crazy how I had absolutely no remembrance of being there the day he was buried. I did not remember the area at all. I had no recollection of getting out of the limo, walking, standing, or being there at all. It didn't look familiar to me in the least. It was if this was the first time I had been there. If you think about it, it basically was the first time. The day of the funeral, I was just a physical form, going through the motions. God had my soul protected in a bubble that day. He was now slowly starting to pop my bubble and was allowing me to feel the pain. I didn't like it, but I knew and understood that for me to heal from this pain, I had to go deep and really feel the pain.

People had always told me that the day will come when the boys will ask to go to the cemetery. I never believed it because I just thought they were too young to ask about going there. Well, I was wrong. The day came when they asked to go. They saw a cemetery on the way home from school one day. They asked if Daddy was in that cemetery. When I told them no and that Daddy's cemetery is by Mamu and Papu's house (my parents), they asked if we could stop there since we were, in fact, heading over to Mamu and Papu's house. I remember thinking to myself, "Really, God? Today is the day?" I asked them if they really wanted to see Daddy's stone. They both exclaimed yes. I thought to myself again, *Okay, God. You better guide this!*

I remember the drive to the cemetery that day very clearly. The boys were full of questions, and it became this amazing teachable moment about God's truths. Zane, who was six at this point, has always been wise beyond his years. He asked if Daddy still looked the way he always looked or is he just bones now since he's buried in the ground. I was as honest with him as I could be. I told him and his brother that Daddy's body is in a casket, which is then in a lined cement vault that helps to protect and preserve bodies from water, dirt, etc., but that it is only natural for things to decompose, including flesh, so I wasn't really sure. He also asked why we bury people in the ground when they die. I told him that God made us from the earth. We started out as dust from the ground, so back to dust we go when we die. I told him that God teaches us that in the Bible. Genesis 3:19 (NLT): "Until you return to the ground, from which you were made. For you were dust, and to dust you will return."

Zane also told me about a dream he had often with Daddy in it. He told me how Daddy would come through his door and just look at him. Zane said he asked him what he was doing here because he thought he was dead. He said that Daddy never said anything. He just watched him. I told Zane that perhaps God allows Daddy to visit him in his dreams so that you know that Daddy has not, and never will, forget him. Zane talked about how he can still have Daddy in his dreams, and Xavier chimed in with he can still have Daddy in his heart. I remember not crying because Zane said it always made him feel weird when I cried. I didn't want him to feel weird. I don't remember even having the feeling of wanting to cry. I remember having the feeling of gratitude that I had such an amazing conversation with my boys and the opportunity to answer as honestly as I could. I always believed in and still believe in honest and upfront answers. No foo-foo feel-good answers. God's answers are the feel-good answers because they are truth.

When we reached the cemetery, I was as calm as could be. It was surprising since this was only the second time I had been there myself. But I was. I was peaceful. I was at ease. We got out of the car, and the boys ran to Mark's headstone. They were running their fingers over Mark's name, over my name, over the engraved plane and lighthouse. They had questions as to why my name was on there. Zane already knew why my name didn't have an ending date.

Xavier asked if Daddy could just bust up through the ground. Of course, I told him no and explained why that couldn't happen. We had discussions about how our earthly bodies with skin are basically shells and how our internal soul is the core to who we really are. Our earthly bodies with skin get buried, but our souls go on to heaven to be with Jesus. We prayed at the stone thanking Jesus for being the reason that Daddy gets to live forever in heaven. We thanked Him for being the reason that we will see Daddy again one day when we live in heaven. I remember just sitting back and watching Zane and Xavier with awe. They were running all around. Zane was even recording; they were looking at other stones and commenting on names and dates. They weren't sad. They weren't angry. They were curious. They were joyful. They were filled with peace. I watched how they smiled and how they laughed. And I heard God tell me, "See. I guided this!"

I learned that day that God will always provide the perfect timing for the boys to conquer milestones as well. God reveals truths to them when He knows that their little minds and souls can handle it. I learned that day that He allows me to conquer milestones when my mind and soul can handle it as well. I don't ever need to feel pressured or hurried to conquer something. I don't ever need to feel like I must respond to things in a certain way or rush my grieving. I don't ever need to feel as if I must force my boys into conquering hurdles. I sit back and let God lead it. There is a time and a place for everything to happen. That time and place is when and where God says it is.

I must be honest and add that there have been several times where I wanted to speed the grieving process up because I just want it done with. However, if I forced it to be done on my timeline, it wouldn't be healthy. I wouldn't conquer and complete with the peace that I have had because my soul wouldn't have been ready to handle it. God knows me better than I know myself. Romans 8:27–37 says,

> And the Father who knows all hearts knows what the Spirit is saying, for the Spirit pleads for us believers in harmony with God's own will. And we know that God causes everything to work together for the good of those who love God and are called according to his purpose for them. (NLT)

He knows when my heart can handle things. To listen to my own timeline would only set me back, hinder my healing, and cause me unnecessary and additional pain. This is true to my present day as I continue to heal. It took me five and half years to finally clean out Mark's closet. It was a daunting task looming over me for a while. I had some people even make the statement that I should have had that cleaned out by now. *No!* I should not have.

When I finally did so, I did so with great peace. It was as if I was cleaning out any ordinary closet. It was as if Jesus Himself had His hands on mine as I took each item off the hanger, off the shelf, folded them up, and put them into boxes. I did not shed one tear. I did not have one ounce of sadness. I smiled remembering Mark wearing certain things. When I was done, and the closet was completely empty, I stood in the middle of it and laughed. I remember dancing in the closet and exclaiming; "I did it. I did it. I am free. I am free." I'm not sure what I was free from. Free from the weight of knowing that closet had to be conquered? I'm not sure. But I had a feeling of freedom. Would I have felt this way if I had cleaned his closet out any sooner? I do not believe for a second that I would have. It would have been an incredibly emotional, painful, and traumatic experience.

God wanted me to clean it the day that I did and not a day sooner. I will never listen to what people think I should do. I trust God to lead me. I suppose what I mean by saying I enjoy parts of my healing process is that I mean I love how I feel when I conquer milestones with God's guidance. I am left with such an experience of growth and closeness to God that it leaves me just waiting and wanting the next experience to happen. It leaves me wanting to conquer the next painful milestone, because I know the pain is going to be replaced with the mystery of unexplainable peace and a sense of great empowerment and strength. It leaves me speechless and awestruck every time.

CHAPTER 7

Calling on My Significant Other

Sometimes there is no explanation as to why some things happen. Sometimes events happen, and there is no explanation except that it was divine. This is the case about a gift I had received just a few weeks after the accident. I was feeling relatively peaceful one day in late June, so I decided to go and get my hair done. As I sat in that salon chair, waiting for the hairstylist to come back with my hair color, I received a text message. "Call your significant other," it read. I became very anxious, confused, and angry too. Who on earth would send me a message saying something like that? So cruel. There was no real callback number. There was just a long, random number listed that consisted mostly of zeros. No name was listed as to who sent it. A three-digit number (154) in parentheses appeared at the top of my phone. I first tried to text back, asking who this was. It came back with red Xs and a message that said, "Message error. Cannot send." I tried several more times to text back and every time, I received those same red Xs with the same "Message error. Cannot send" message. I sat there completely bewildered and very distraught.

The hairstylist came back with my hair color and began working on my hair. I tried calling Mark's cell phone. After all, it did say to call my significant other. It went straight to his voice mail. I tried to call the so-called callback number with the tons of zeros. I simply received the message "Your call cannot be completed as dialed." I frantically tried to figure out what the 154 number in parentheses was. I searched the phone extensively for some indication of what this number meant. I finally discovered that in the main menu of my phone, where there was a collection of all my old, previous voice mails, I found the dates and times these voice mails were left, and next to each one was the number 154 in parentheses.

At this point my head was spinning. I could not, for the life of me, figure out where this text message came from. I had no idea who sent it. I could not even begin to imagine that someone would send me something like that. The thing is that no one would have sent me such a text message. I wanted the hairstylist to just finish up my hair so I could leave and try to find answers. I thought I could go to the Verizon store and maybe they could help me by looking into my account. So I sat there for two hours, waiting for her to finish.

I shared with her what was happening, and she probably thought I was nuts. I told her how Mark just died a couple of weeks ago, and she was convinced that Mark had sent me the message. I wanted to believe that, but I'm not so quick to believe in such things; however, the feeling of being frozen in a moment and the sensation that overcame me while I was waiting for the hairstylist to return clearly points that something that is truly out of this world was taking place.

It took her two hours to do my hair. It felt like the longest two hours in the world. I quickly paid, and after I left the salon, I raced to the Verizon store. I approached the man in the Verizon store and tried to appear calm and normal. He had no idea who I was. He had no idea of what just happened in my life. I showed him my phone. I showed him how I received this text from an unknown source and that I am unable to text it back. I showed him the weird callback number and asked what the 154 in parenthesis meant. He looked at me very puzzled. He looked at the phone and tried to text back himself, and, again, the same red Xs and "Message error. Cannot send" showed up. He simply said to me; "Hmmm? I really don't know. This is weird. I have never seen this before."

I thanked him for trying, and I left the store completely beside myself. My next thought was to call Mark's brother. He was good at being able to find things out that had to do with cell phones, technology, etc. So I called him and told him what was going on. He accessed my Verizon account online. He knew how to locate the information that revealed all my incoming and outgoing texts and the times that they were sent. He could tell me who I sent messages to and who sent them to me. There was absolutely no notification whatsoever about a text that said, "Call your significant other." It was as if it was never sent. But it was. I had it on my phone. He also located the number 154 and said it had something to do with my voice mail on the phone account, but it was something that messages via text could not be sent to or from.

I was starting to be convinced that Mark sent me a text from heaven. When I got home, I immediately charged up Mark's phone.

I searched his phone. I went through all his voice mail messages, all his text messages, and of course there was no indication that this text message that I had received came from his phone. The interesting thing that I did find, though, was in his main menu, where it showed the history of his old voice mail messages, the 154 number, in parentheses, was located next to each voice mail message. Just like it appeared in mine. When I canceled our joint cell phone plan, canceled Mark's phone number, and entered into a single cell phone plan just for me, the code 154 was no longer anywhere to be seen. That number was a code that was unique to our joint cell phone plan. And I was now convinced, more than ever, that Mark was trying to contact me.

Before I get into the truth that was later revealed to me about that text message, let me go back and explain that sensation of being frozen in time in the hair salon before my hairstylist returned. I sat there, trying so hard to figure out where this text message had come from. I was searching my phone, trying to call numbers, trying to figure out some logical explanation when, suddenly, I just stopped. I just looked up at the ceiling, and calm just washed over me. I had tears streaming from my eyes, and I remember whispering the words "It's all okay. It's all about love. I just feel love. Pure and perfect love. It's all about 100 percent, pure, perfect, and total love. It's all okay. It's more than okay." I remember looking around me, and it was as if things were frozen. People were there, moving slowly, but I heard no noise. I felt nothing but *love*. It was beautiful beyond explanation, and it was different. We all experience that feeling of love, and there are many ways to love. We know how it feels to love our spouses or significant others. We know how to love our parents, family, and friends. If we have children, we know how to love our children. And to me, being a woman who has given birth to two children, I believe that there is no stronger bond or love that you can have than that love between a mother and child. But this love that I was feeling in that hair salon was stronger than all those kinds of love put together. It was crazy powerful. It was a moment frozen in time for me. It lasted for about thirty to forty-five seconds, and then I was back in the reality of the day.

I cannot explain it. No words can explain what I felt that day. I know that it really does sound crazy, but I truly believe that I was given the opportunity to feel the true, unconditional, unselfish, all perfect, all pure love of Christ that day. No other love is more perfect and purer than the love of Jesus Christ. Any love we feel on earth is tainted and can be selfish. That's just humanness. But with Christ it is impossible to experience any falseness, anything masked, or anything but pure and perfect love.

To really love someone is to not have butterflies in the stomach. True love is to stand out. It's to forgive others when you feel wronged. It's truly the desire of wanting the well-being for another person. It's praying for someone to be guided by God and to be directed down a path that transforms him or her into the person that God intends for that individual to be. Love is not an emotion that lessens or dissipates over time, due to circumstances. If you truly love someone, it is surrendered to God. It's powerful. It's unconditional. It's greater beyond anything comprehensible. True love is eternal. And true, eternal love comes from one place and one place alone. It comes from Jesus Christ.

There is no fear in true love. If there is fear, then it is not from God. First John 4:18 says, "There is no fear in love. But perfect love drives out fear, because fear has to do with punishment. The one who fears is not made perfect in love" (NIV). This is the love that I felt that day for that short amount of time. I had no fear. I had no sadness. I had nothing but pure and perfect love that overwhelmed my soul. I sat there whispering those words to the ceiling. If anyone saw me, I am sure that they thought I had lost my mind.

Again, I know it sounds crazy. It sounds far-fetched. I cannot explain it in a way to capture the extraordinary sensations that overcame me that day. It's okay if there are people who think I have experienced momentary insanity because I know what I felt that day, and it was real. It was a gift. It remains a gift to this day, which was revealed to me to help me grow and apply a Christ type of love to my relationships. I believe God wants to teach me that loving others is not about me. I truly believe, without a doubt, that God allowed me to feel, just for seconds that day, what it is like to feel love in heaven, and that is what Mark gets to feel 24/7. First Corinthians 13:4–7 is probably the most known scripture on love, and it's beautiful. It is used in wedding ceremonies all the time and rightfully so. I used it at mine and, honestly, really didn't understand the depth of that scripture. When I read it now, after experiencing what I did that day in the hair salon, it takes on a completely different meaning, and that is a gift! "Love is patient, love is kind. It does not envy, it does not boast, it is not proud. It does not dishonor others, it is not self-seeking, it is not easily angered, it keeps no record of wrongs. Love does not delight in evil but rejoices with the truth. It always protects, always trusts, always hopes, always perseveres" (NIV).

So, for a while, I was convinced that the text message of "call your significant other" was indeed from Mark. He was my significant other, and for a long time after he died, I felt as if he still was my significant other. There was no other explanation, and I took comfort in it. However, as time passed, God revealed the truth behind that text message. I never did find any evidence of who it came from. At least from anybody on earth, and to this day it remains a mystery. But not really. It doesn't remain a mystery to those who see with the eyes of their hearts.

I began to realize that I still had a significant other, but it wasn't Mark. Mark had passed on, and God was teaching me that our loved ones who go home to Him do not try to contact us. In 2 Corinthians we are taught that when we die, we go immediately to heaven—"absent from the body, present with the Lord." Nowhere in the Bible are we taught that we are to call on our loved ones for guidance. Nowhere in the Bible are we taught that our loved ones intercede for us. We are taught, however, that it is Christ who we call on for guidance. It is Christ who intercedes for us. We are not to pray to our loved ones. We pray to Christ, who takes our prayers to the Father. Psalm 50:15 tells us to call upon Him: "Then call on me when you are in trouble, and I will rescue you and you will give me glory" (NLT). Romans 8:34 states: "Who then is the one who condemns? No one. Christ Jesus who died, more than that, who was raised to life, who is at the right hand of God, and is also interceding for us" (NIV).

Mark didn't die and rise to life for me. Jesus did. Jesus died and rose for Mark. That's why Mark is in heaven to begin with. Mark is powerless to have any influence over my earthly life. The only way he can influence me is by me thinking, *What would Mark do? How would Mark handle circumstances?* I can only seek Mark's guidance by remembering the kind of person he was, by remembering his character, his abilities. But to seek him out, to pray to him, to want him to watch over me, I don't believe it's biblical for him to do so. I believe that Mark is not concerned with things of this world. He has graduated to the kingdom of God where there is no sadness, no stress, no worries, and no pain. For Mark to be "keeping in touch" with me would mean he's not free from the pain of this broken world. The earth is a broken world. Heaven is not. He can't be between two realms. And honestly, why would I want that? That would be truly selfish on my part. I don't want Mark here. I want him there, with Jesus, feeling that pure and perfect love 24/7. Revelation 21:4 reveals that our sorrow is gone forever: "He will wipe every tear from their eyes, and there will be no more death or sorrow or crying or pain. All these things are gone forever" (NLT). If Mark is watching over me, then that would make that scripture a lie. Scripture is the living word of God. I would be calling God a liar, and God is not a liar.

So I have learned to call on my significant other—my significant other who is Jesus Christ. He is more significant than any earthly significant other could ever be. He is the only significant other that can hear you, cry with you, hold you, carry you, heal you, and save you. He will do anything for you, if it's according to His will for you, if you just call on Him. I've learned that in John 14:13, I can pray to Jesus, not Mark, and ask Him to wrap His arms around Mark and tell him it's from me. "You can ask for anything in my name, and I will do it, so that the Son can bring glory to the Father" (NLT). I take that to mean that I can pray and ask Jesus to tell Mark I love him, I miss him, ask Him to hug Mark, ask Him to let Mark know about something, and I believe He does that for me. I no longer believe it was Mark sending me that text message that day. I believe it was Jesus Christ. I believe He wanted me to know that

Mark is safe, home with Him, and wanted me to know how he now experiences love. It was in His timing that He revealed to me just who my real significant other is, and that truth is what brings me real, solid comfort that can never be taken away.

CHAPTER 8

God Is Real, but So Is Satan

Death has a way of driving a wedge between you and the people you love the most. It seems it should be the opposite. You should want to cling to the people you love and trust the most. For the most part, that is true; however, when someone closest to you dies, the grief of it tends to isolate you. That was certainly the case with me, just a couple of months after the accident. I was probably the most depressed and most stricken with grief then. It was now August, and up until this point I was giving myself the pep talks of "I've got this! God is with me. He is showing me the way. I am strong."

It was right around this time that the cards and letters were dwindling in the mail. Even though it took me months to eventually go through the hundreds and hundreds of cards and letters that came, when they stopped coming in the mail, it was almost a letdown. In some strange way, I looked forward to seeing how many I would get each day, and I loved chucking them into a pile.

The daily phone calls were stopping too. Again, even though I wouldn't answer a lot of them, or even call back, the phone ringing and people's voice mails were somehow a comfort to me. On one hand I hated the voice mails reminding me that Mark died. Then when they were coming to an end, I got angry with thoughts of *Doesn't anybody care anymore?* I know. I totally contradicted myself. But nothing about the death of Mark made sense in those early months or even those first couple of years.

It takes a long time for any rhyme or reason to surface. So people were continuing with their lives. The death of Mark affected so many but not in the way it did for the boys and me. It was normal for so many people to go weeks, even months at a time without seeing or speaking to Mark. But me? The boys? Our daily lives were interrupted.

There was no more normal routine of Mark coming through the garage door and instantly tackling the boys to the ground. There was no more of the normal sound of his work shoes clicking on the kitchen floor in the morning as he headed out to work. There was no more normal routine of Mark gradually waking up in the morning, sitting on the edge of the bed, and me snuggling into him after I got out of the shower. All our daily routines were wiped away. Gone. Never to return. Everyone else's daily lives carried on as normal. Not for us three. We were forever "abnormal." So at least I thought for a long time.

I hit rock bottom that August. All my daily pep talks and positive thoughts of "I'm strong and I've got this," faded, and I sank. I sank hard, and I sank deep. I reached a point that I did not want anyone around me. I would ignore the calls from the people that did consistently call me. I didn't even want the boys around me. I wanted no help, and I certainly did not want to be hugged, held, or coddled, and that is exactly what my mother wanted to do. My mother was a saint and still is. When I ask her now what I did with the boys during that time, she simply tells me that she had them most of that summer. She said I was gone a lot. I don't know what I did but I wasn't around the boys much, it seems. She wanted to hug me and cry with me, and I didn't want it. To be honest, she was getting on my nerves. I felt smothered by her. I was overwhelmed by her. It's crazy how much I needed her and counted on her but didn't want her around.

She is my mother. She wanted to take away all the pain and fix my world, but no one could fix this. Not even Mom. No one could take away the pain. Not even God could at this point, so certainly not my mother. My mother was pretty much at my house constantly up until this point. I had, however, reached the point that I needed her to go. We got into a huge fight one afternoon, and I told her she needed to leave because I wanted to be alone. She listened and stayed away. We talk about that time now, and the hurt, the pain she felt as a mother that day, cannot be explained in words. She said she remembers feeling like a failure because as my mother, it was her job to fix this for me, and she couldn't do it. She stayed away for a while, and she will tell you to this day that she does not remember any part of that time. It's a lost time in her life.

So here I was, alone with my thoughts, alone with the boys, alone in the deepest valley with no way out. I started to drive myself crazy with the thought of just wanting to see Mark. I struggled. I racked my brain for some place to go so that I could be close to him. I thought about the cemetery and didn't want to really go there because he wasn't there. I thought about going to the airport hangar, where Mark and his best friend kept their plane. That wouldn't work either. He wouldn't be there.

I remember my dad coming by the one day. All I kept saying to him was that I couldn't find any place to go so that I could be close to Mark. There was nowhere to go. He was hugging me, and he told me that I didn't need to go anywhere because he (Mark) was right there, and he pointed to my heart. I cried and cried and just kept saying there was no way out. I just wanted to be next to Mark, and there was absolutely no way that could be accomplished. It's hard to describe. I felt as if I was in this room that was completely enclosed. I would just run around the perimeter of it trying to desperately break through the walls to a perfect path that led to Mark. Only I never broke through it. It was sealed solid, and there was absolutely no path to Mark. Or was there? Was there a path to Mark who had *died*? Mark was dead, and I so desperately wanted to be close to him. I so desperately wanted the boys to have their father, so I was determined to take them to him. I figured out what the perfect path to Mark was. I wanted it to be physically painless for us to take this path, so I had thought of the perfect route.

I gathered up the boys' favorite blankets, favorite pillows, and favorite stuffed animals. We were going to have a party in the car. The car that would be turned on and totally enclosed in the garage. I planned on turning on the music so we could dance and sing. Then we could snuggle up and just fall asleep. I was convinced that I was just taking me and the boys to be with their daddy and that there was nothing wrong with that. We would close our eyes, with no pain, no knowledge, and when we opened them again, Daddy would be there, holding out his arms, and we could run into them. Nothing was wrong with what I was doing. God should have taken all three of us to begin with. To think that the boys and I could live here on this earth without Mark was just plain stupid and wrong. I was taking matters into my own hands and fixing this. To Daddy we were going, and there was nothing wrong with that.

I had Xavier in my arms and Zane at my side, along with our blankets and stuffed animals. We were just steps away from opening the door that led to the garage when my doorbell rang. I happened to be standing right in front of my front door, so I couldn't help but see who was ringing my doorbell. As I looked out, I saw my neighbor, who was waving to me. I remember thinking, *Ugh! He sees me, and he knows I see him. Now I have to answer!* So I did answer the door. He was taking care of my lawn that summer, and he needed something from the shed that was in the back of the house. Well, I totally got interrupted from heading down my path to Mark, and so obviously and thankfully, I never took that path to completion.

It was not a coincidence that my neighbor showed up at my door when he did. My neighbor didn't know what was going on with me inside my house that day, but God sure did. I truly believe that God sent my neighbor to my house, at that exact time, right when we would see each other through the window, providing an opportunity that I had to answer the doorbell, to save me from the hold that Satan had on me that day.

In 2 Timothy 4:18, we are told that God will rescue His children from attacks by Satan: "The Lord will rescue me from every evil attack and will bring me safely to His Heavenly Kingdom. To Him be glory forever and ever. Amen" (NIV). I was truly rescued that day. When I look back at my train of thought that day, I now see how manipulated my thoughts were. I wanted to take my own life.

I wanted to take the lives of my children. I would have committed suicide and murder all at the same time!

I was convinced, or I should say that Satan had convinced me, that all I was doing was taking us to Daddy. The evil one had me thinking that there was nothing wrong with that. How sick and twisted that thought really is! That is what Satan does. He takes something that is so sick and twisted, manipulates it, and presents it as a wonderful and loving thing. Satan will come and prey on your darkest hours. He will rob you of joy. He will play with your mind and warp your thinking. He will make you doubt God's promises. He will whisper in your ear that God has destroyed your life and that He cannot be trusted. He will bring you to rock bottom and convince you that the most wicked of ways are truly the most wonderful ways. He can disguise anything to look attractive. He can disguise even himself. "And no wonder, for even Satan disguises himself as an angel of light" (2 Corinthians 11:14 NIV). Satan even tried to tempt Jesus in the wilderness with "deals" too good to be true. "Again, the devil took Him to a very high mountain and showed Him all the kingdoms of the world and their splendor. All this I will give to you, he said, if you will bow down and worship me. Jesus said to him, away from me Satan! For it is written 'Worship the Lord your God and serve Him only'" (Matthew 4:8–10 NIV). Of course, Jesus wouldn't fall for the tricks of Satan. But for us, as humans, we can, unfortunately. Especially when your mind is stuck in hardcore misery and grief like mine was.

It wasn't until later, after some time when this situation had passed, that I realized for the first time just how powerful and *real* Satan is. I always believed in God, so sure, I guess I believed in Satan too. I never gave it much thought and, honestly, thought people were kind of crazy for putting emphasis on Satan. But now having experienced what I did that day in August of 2010, I, without a doubt, believe in the power of Satan. God is real, but so is Satan. He is very real but, thankfully, my foundation for Christ was already established. I am His child, and He was not going to allow me to fall victim to Satan. Satan and the battle between good and evil are very real. The spiritual realm of God and His angels versus Satan and his demons is something I believe to be as true as the grass is green.

Satan may be real, and he may be powerful, but the good news is that God is real and more powerful than Satan could ever be. Satan is already destroyed. He was destroyed the day Christ died on the cross. Satan may try his hardest, and unfortunately there will be souls that succumb to his evil. However, for those of us who are cemented in Christ, as hard as Satan tries, he can never win over our souls. The strength and power of Christ crushes Satan every single time, and the time is coming when He will crush the evil one once and for all. "The God of peace will soon crush Satan under your feet" (Romans 16:20 NIV). God crushed Satan that day when I almost ended my life and the lives of my boys. I have never been to that point ever again.

CHAPTER 9

Angels at Christmastime

God sent me a lot of messages that first year after Mark went home. One message I truly believe He wanted me to see and understand is that His spiritual resources are always at work. We can't always see that with our naked, human eye, but with the eyes of faith we must believe until the day comes when we can see with our physical eyes. It was November, just six months after Mark had died. I found a book about angels. I am always skeptical to read books about angels. So many of them are written from man's perspective of what angels are and what they are capable of. So many times, angel books are not based off biblical scripture. For me, in order to believe anything, I must have scripture to back it up. So when I found this one book, I scanned it. It seemed to be pretty much based on scripture. Even the last chapter talked about how it is Jesus Christ who is to be worshipped and not angels. So I bought the book and took it home and read it. The book talked about how God will send His angels for protection, for comfort, or to deliver direct messages. It gave people's accounts of seeing "white, angelic" like things. People described seeing "smoke-like" blurs. People described angels protecting them and giving them remarkable peace. I read through the book, and when I finished it, I slammed it shut, rolled my eyes, tossed it on the floor, and claimed it to be a book of total nonsense. If we have angels that protect us, then where in the world have mine been? So I put the book down and left it at that.

December rolled around, and the dreaded Christmas holiday loomed. It was our first Christmas without Mark, and I didn't want to be here. In fact, I made plans to take the boys to Walt Disney World for Christmas. Plane tickets were bought, hotel reservations were made, and the itinerary was complete. We were not sticking around for Christmas in Ohio. However, I felt that I needed to still put up a tree. It was for two little boys who needed to have a Christmas tree. So on December 10, I put one up. Yes. I remember the exact date. Xavier found this little beer mug key chain that Mark had brought home from somewhere. He hung it on the tree. I thought it was funny, so I wanted to take a picture of it and tell everyone that we decorate our tree with beer mugs. So I was taking pictures of it with my phone/camera. Every time I tried to take the picture, it was all blurry and out of focus. When I would snap the picture, the image was all messed up. I started taking random pictures around the house, and it was the same thing. Every time it was out of focus and blurry, and I would get these funky images when I took the picture. I wasn't even focused on the images that I was taking. All I knew was that they weren't normal pictures, and I was mad because now my phone/camera was broken. It was about an hour later when my phone was finally working totally fine again.

It was exactly one week later, when I finally looked at the images I snapped, that I realized the power and love of God. I was still teaching. I was at school on this day. I was having an over the top, emotional, horrible day. I couldn't teach kids. I couldn't focus on anything. All I could do was find quiet corners in that school building and cry. I had so much anger that day. I was so deep in grief, and I don't know why I was even there that day. But God would prove to me how He uses others to bring attention to what He wants to show you. It was lunchtime, and I was sitting in the teacher's lounge. I was scrolling through my pictures that I took just the week before when I thought my phone was broken. I said to a couple of teacher friends sitting with me, "Hey, you guys. Look at these funky pictures I took on my phone the other day. My phone was all messed up, and this is what I got." (At this point, I still was not seeing what God had given me through these pictures.) As my friends scrolled through them, the one friend said to me, "Shannon, did you look at these? These are angels. How can you not see them?" This was the moment that I was, for the first time, seeing what God wanted me to see.

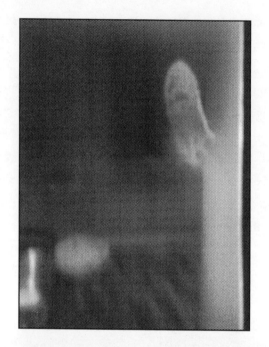

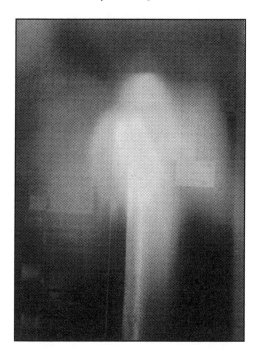

I am certainly not here to tell anyone what to believe about the images on those pictures. You can evaluate them and come to your own conclusion, but for me, I know what they are. I truly believe that God was telling me to trust and believe with the eyes of faith that His angels are hard at work protecting me and my boys and that I do not need to be afraid in such a dire circumstance. I believe He allowed me to see His angels through the snapshots of my phone camera because I was scared to death for my life, my boys' lives, and my future.

So how did I come to this realization? Well, as I have stated before, I need scripture in order to believe that something is truly from God. When I realized exactly what I had in these pictures, I said to God, "Okay, God. If these are in fact pictures of angels, if this is in fact something from you, you need to confirm so. You need to show me or do something to cement this for me." As if the images weren't enough for me to believe. However, God is faithful, and it was just like Him to "cement" this for me. The very next day, my pastor called me, for what he thought, was to just get a phone number for somebody.

When I told him about the pictures I just discovered, he led me to 2 Kings 6:15–17. Here we learn about a servant boy who is afraid when he looks up on a hillside to see an opposing army. "When the servant of the man of God got up early the next morning and went outside, there were troops, horses and chariots everywhere. Oh sir, he said, what will we do now? The young servant man cried to Elisha. Don't be afraid, Elisha told him. For there are more on our side than on theirs. Then Elisha prayed, Oh Lord, open his eyes and let him see. The Lord opened the young man's eyes and when he looked up, he saw that the hillside around Elisha was filled with horses and chariots of fire" (NLT).

I believe God allowed my eyes to be opened to see His heavenly army surrounding me, just as He allowed that servant boy's eyes to be opened. He was afraid and needed to be comforted. I was afraid and needed to be comforted. I was feeling so alone and so scared, and God said, "Look! You are not alone, and you don't need to be afraid." I believe He waited a week after I took the pictures to reveal them to me because that's when I needed to see them the most. I was beside myself that day at school. My emotions were out of control, and it took a couple of teacher friends to bring me to the reality of what was in those pictures. That weekend, after seeing what was really in those pictures, and with the 2 Kings scripture to back this up, I went with my kids and a friend to the Polar Express train ride. For the first time since Mark had died, I did not feel sad and wish that Daddy was there to see his boys. I did not dwell on his death. I was, for the first time, just in the moment. I truly basked in the joy of being with my kids watching them smile and having fun. I was smiling too. I was present without fear, and it was all because He allowed me, for some reason, to see His spiritual resources that are always at work.

I realized that it was God's angels hard at work that kept me from being trapped under the camper too. As you recall from the first chapter, I was standing on the step outside of the camper when it hovered up and flipped over. It flipped over in the direction that Mark and I were standing. It somehow knocked Mark over, but as for me? I went *in* the camper. Why didn't I fall off the step? Why didn't the camper fall on top of me too? It doesn't logically make sense to me that I went in instead of falling off the step when that was the way the camper was flipping over.

I truly believe that angels, the same ones I have pictures of, pushed me in and trapped my foot. "For He will command His angels concerning you, to guard you in all your ways. They will lift you up with their hands, so that you will not strike your foot against a stone" (Psalm 91:11–12 NIV). My foot suffered a great injury. The camper door slammed on it. It was throbbing and bleeding. It stayed stuck until help arrived. I could not walk on it for a few days. I thought it was truly gone. But not one single bone was broken. Not even one.

When I stop and think about everything that was taking place in the spiritual realm when the camper flipped, my mind simply can't comprehend it all. Jesus and His angels were rescuing Mark by escorting him into the heavenly realm, all while He and His angels were protecting me from death by pushing me inside the camper.

Concerning the boys, Jesus and His angels were keeping the two of them safe as they fell backward. I don't know how it all works, but I can only hope that one day that moment can be played for me, like a movie, just so I can see how it all happened.

When my teacher friends pointed out that I had angels in these pictures, one thing that was said to me was: "That's Mark. He's looking over you because he's now your guardian angel." Although I know that people mean well when they say that, it really brings me no comfort, and that's because it simply isn't true. I know that those pictures are not Mark, and they are not from Mark. If we are Christ followers and believe in the Word of God, we know that we do not die and become angels. Angels are separate creatures created by God since the beginning of time to carry out His plans—His will.

Hebrews 12:22–23 helps us to understand that when we enter heaven we will be greeted by different groups. These groups are angels and spirits of God's children who have gotten to heaven before us. "You have come to Mount Zion, to the city of the living God, the heavenly Jerusalem, and to countless thousands of angels in a joyful gathering. You have come to the assembly of God's firstborn children whose names are written in heaven. You have come to God Himself who is the judge over all things. You have come to the spirits of righteous ones in heaven who have now been made perfect" (NLT).

We will never find scripture to back up the notion that we die and become angels. In fact, scripture teaches us that although we are lower than angels as we live our earthly lives, once we die and enter heaven, we will judge angels. "Do you not know that we will judge angels? How much more the things of this life?" (1 Corinthians 6:3 NIV).

It's always tempting to believe something that sounds nice and comforting, but if we are going to believe something that is contradictory to scripture, I think it does the opposite of comfort. It's not truth. Truth is what comforts. Truth puts us on a path of healing. I don't think we can pick and choose what is true in the Bible.

We can't manipulate or twist the words of scripture to conform to what we want to be true either. Everything must be held accountable to scripture. So what about those areas that aren't so black and white in the Bible? What do we do with that? Does that exist? I absolutely believe that there are indeed gray areas.

I think all we can do with that is formulate our opinions and thoughts to the best of our biblical knowledge and understanding, and we could be wrong in those opinions. If you debate with someone about a topic, know that you could be wrong, or the other person could be wrong, or you both could be wrong. I don't believe God's word is meant to have multiple interpretations. Sometimes we just don't know what everything means, and we must be willing to say, "I may have it wrong."

So while I get why people want to tell me Mark is my guardian angel and is now watching over me, I just simply don't believe it, therefore it brings no comfort. That's not what scripture teaches me, and it's God's word that brings me true comfort. Is it possible that God let Mark know that He was going to allow me to see His spiritual resources all around my tree? I don't know. Does God let our loved ones know what His plans are concerning us who were left behind on earth? I'm not sure.

Perhaps that's a gray area we can only speculate about. Perhaps that's an area where we don't have to put God in a box and dare to believe that He can and will do whatever He wants without having to let us in on every little detail of His sovereignty. All I know is that God gave me a gift that day—a gift of His angels sent to my house to show me that I am protected. I am loved. I am not forgotten. I am not alone.

I can only imagine what it must be like to see His angels like that with your actual naked eye. Surely it would be too much for our human minds to witness and see while on earth, so He allowed me the next best thing—pictures taken with what I thought was a broken camera. Pictures about a month later after reading a book about angels that I called nonsense. When I angrily said out loud after reading that book, "If we have angels, then where in the world have mine been?" little did I know that in just a few weeks God would basically say, "Here ya go, ya little brat! Here are your angels!" I am forever in awe of such a once in a lifetime gift!

CHAPTER 10

Sacred Ground

Upon returning home after that dreadful weekend, I made the statement that I would never set foot on that campground again. In fact, I wanted it wiped off the earth and couldn't imagine anyone ever wanting to go there after learning what had happened to my family there. I called it the ugliest place imaginable. But a strange thing happened as I was approaching the first anniversary of Mark's death. God basically told me, "You are going back to that campground on the one-year anniversary." I tried to push the thought out of my head, but I heard it loud and clear. I was being told to go. I had a lot of people worried about me going back there and could not understand how I could even think about going back to such a horrific place. As much as I tried to tune out the voice of God, I couldn't. So I listened. I made the journey back up to the campground in Pennsylvania. I can tell you, without a doubt, I absolutely did the right thing.

One of my most loved and dearest friends, Lisa, went with me that first year. She suggested that we should go up the day before and sleep over at a place called Geneva-on-the-Lake, Ohio, which is only thirty minutes away from the campground. She suggested we go, relax, and make it more like a celebration. I thought it was a great idea, so that's exactly what we did. We went up the day before and stayed over in a lodge. We drank wine, ate good food, swam in the pool, drank wine, vegged in the hot tub, drank wine, reminisced, drank wine, visited wineries, you get the picture. It was a brilliant idea. It helped to take the edge off the anxiousness I had about where I was headed the next day.

The next day arrived. *The* day—June 6, 2011, exactly one year after Mark had died. We got to the campground rather late in the afternoon. We took our time getting up, had breakfast, and went out of our way to visit another winery. I think Lisa knew to just take it easy. I think she knew I needed to take my time, and she knew how to take all the pressure off. There were no time constraints or rules on how this needed to be done. We just went with the flow, and eventually we journeyed on our way to the campground.

It was strange to travel the path to the campground again. I was reflecting, and while I could remember certain landmarks along the way, a lot of it was so unfamiliar. Mark was doing the driving that day, so I wasn't paying a whole lot of attention as we maneuvered our way to that campground. So much of the way was forgotten to me. However, when we approached the little stone roadway that led to the main house at the campground, my memory was suddenly fully intact. We pulled up, and I remember stopping the car approximately five hundred feet from that main house. I just stared straight ahead at that main house. It's where we checked in. I remembered where Mark had parked. I remembered waiting in the car while he ran in to get things settled. I couldn't breathe.

Seriously, I couldn't breathe. I had a huge lump in my throat, and I literally could not get air in and out. Lisa and I sat there for a bit. I don't think I was crying yet. I just hyperventilated. Eventually, I did drive that last five hundred feet. The owners of the campground came out and welcomed me with open arms.

Honestly, I can't remember much of the conversation I had with the owners that first year revisiting the campground. I know we talked a lot. What does stand out to me about our conversation is what she told me Mark had said to her. When Mark went into the main office to change the site we were going to put the camper on, he was asked if we were going to stay one night or two nights. His reply was, "Well, for now we are staying for one night, but if I survive these storms, we will stay for two." Oh, how I wish I could ask him what made him say that. Did he know storms were coming? Was he paying attention to the weather on his phone? Did he sense patterns of a storm just by looking at the sky? I have no idea why he would have said that. He never once made any comment to me that he thought a storm was headed our way. I am sure he wouldn't have kept us there if he thought we were in any kind of danger. It's one of those strange things that I will never know an answer to.

After talking with the owners for a while, I revisited the campground. When I say revisit, I mean I literally revisited every memory that I possibly could. I walked on and touched the dirt on the little playground where the boys and I played cars in the dirt. I looked up at the trees in a wooded area and remembered Mark barreling down the hill, through the trees with Zane. When I walked over to the actual site that our camper was on, I had a hard time identifying which one it was exactly. Every year, when I revisit the campground, I question where our camper was assigned that night. Every year, I always go with the site that is one over to the right of the number that we were assigned. It just always feels right to move over.

So that first year, I tried to replay where the camper was. I replayed where I would have stood on that outside step. I envisioned looking to my right and seeing Mark working fast to get that awning down. As morbid as it may sound, I had to lie down, on my stomach, face directly in the ground in the exact spot and in the exact way that Mark's body had fallen. I cried. I'm talking ugly, gut-wrenching sobs.

Lisa hugged me as I cried. I don't think I could have cried any harder. I talked to Mark. I told him how sorry I was that this happened to him. I wondered what it felt like for him in those last few moments. Did he know he was in trouble? Did he know that he was going to die? Did he see the camper flip? Was he facing away from the camper and had no idea it was flipping?

From what I understand, the camper or something hit him in the back of the head, and then he fell. I know every single detail of that night—all except seeing him fall. I have no idea how he fell. I struggled with that for a long time but eventually came to the belief that God was in fact protecting my eyes from seeing the image of Mark falling and of the camper falling on top of him.

I did find out later, from the family who rescued the boys and myself, how he was laying, exactly, once the camper was lifted. I found out that his body was lying parallel to Lake Erie. He was stomach down, face directly in the grass. He had no dirt under his nails and no sign of a struggle trying to breathe or get up. When his body was turned over, he had just a little bit of blood from his forehead. Other than that, he looked perfectly like Mark.

I have concluded that Mark was in fact hit in the back of the head so hard that he was knocked out and down before he even knew that camper was coming down upon him. I honestly believe that God spared him any physical pain and suffering and that he had no idea that he was suffocating when the camper fell on him. That was the cause of death, by the way, as indicated on the death certificate—compressional asphyxiation—which is the technical term for basically suffocating. I believe he had no idea that he was suffocating. He was knocked out so hard he had no idea. At least this is what I choose to believe. I believe God spared him knowing he was suffocating. I believe God spared me that horrible image. I believe Jesus and His angels were already there escorting him home.

As I lay there in that grass, in the way I could picture Mark's body lying, I wondered what it must have felt like for Mark to be escorted by Jesus and His angels. Did Mark have conflicting feelings between total bliss and just wanting to go with Him, or was he torn knowing he was leaving his wife and kids behind? I wondered if he knew that he very well may have protected the boys and myself by getting the awning down before it flipped, so that it didn't serve as a sail in the high winds. I wondered if he knew that it was because of his suggestion to put the boys in the middle of the camper as we waited out the storm that they were protected in that flip because they landed in a place, against cushions, that prevented them from getting even a scratch on them. I wondered if he heard me screaming, heard the boys screaming. I wondered if he witnessed the angels pushing me in and protecting me from death.

After some time, I got up from the ground and wanted to walk the path that we walked as a family down the rocky shore of Lake Erie. When Lisa and I got there, I had to throw rocks in just like we did that day. I picked up the biggest ones that I could to toss in just like Mark did that day. I wanted to make the big Daddy splashes he did. I collected some rocks to bring back home. I made my way up the stairs from the rocky shore and I continued to walk the way we did, as much as I could remember anyway. I walked over to Gretchen's camper and envisioned myself there again. (Her family's camper is there year-round, so the actual camper was there.) I stood on her steps and looked over in the direction where our camper would have been. It was so surreal that I was back at that spot. Being at this campground was all surreal.

I walked back over to "our site" and stood around the fire ring just like I did that night. I could see the boys chasing each other in the open grassy area. I could see Gretchen sitting in her swing at her camper, starting a fire herself. I sat back down in the grass where Mark's body had lain, and this time I wasn't crying such sad tears. I cried, but now it was a peaceful cry. It was a beautiful, sunny, and warm day that first revisit to the campground. I closed my eyes and put my face toward heaven, and I felt the warmth of the sun that day. I thought about all the events of that entire weekend, from start to finish, even before we got there, and I had an overwhelming sense of God's presence through me. Every single detail of that weekend was so perfectly orchestrated that there is no other explanation except that God's hands were in all of this! Every detail, down to Mark canceling where we were originally planning to go because there were storms for that area. Seriously? He canceled going there because of severe thunderstorms, and we were led to a place where an unexpected tornado ripped through and flipped our camper over in one-hundred-mph winds? I thought about the fact that we were the only thing in that entire campground that was affected by that storm. Nothing else in that entire campground was touched by that tornado except for us (except for a tree limb that was struck). Do you know how many times I have said we should have stayed on the site that was first assigned to us, because then we wouldn't have been hit? Or would we have? Knowing that Mark said "if I survive these storms" to the owner when we first arrived just screams to me that this was all God, just leading us to that particular site, at that particular campground to meet Him at the appointment of all appointments. Mark's divine appointment to meet *Jesus* face to face and be taken home to his *heavenly* zip code. It was an appointment that just was not ever meant to be missed. When it's our time, it's our time. God knows that time, and there is no getting out of that. We cannot add any days to our lives. Our days are determined, and when our earthly days are up, Jesus swoops in and transitions you to *home.* "You have decided the length of our lives. You know how many months we will live, and we are not given a minute longer" (Job 14:5 NLT).

I had such an overwhelming sense of peace come over me as I sat back down in that grass. I just kept whispering, "It's all okay." I looked around at this campground and knew that we were not in the wrong place at the wrong time. In fact, it was just the opposite. We were in the right place at the right time. God led us to this beautiful place that overlooks Lake Erie. It was a blessing for all four of us to be together when God took Mark's soul home. You are supposed to be with your spouse for their most important events in their life. Earthly death is no different.

I was there. I know how it all happened. All the details from start to finish are etched in my mind—all except seeing Mark fall, that is. Again, God protected my eyes from such a horrifying image. I looked around at that campground and smiled. A place that I thought would forever be a horrific and ugly place of tragedy has been transformed into a sacred place of ultimate beauty. It is the place where Mark's soul went home, and there is nothing more beautiful than that. It's the closest that I can get to heaven, and it's glorious.

When I left the campground that day, I had the feeling of belonging there. It felt as if I had come home. It's the only place on earth where I can get as close to heaven as I can. When I got home that day, I told my mom that it was so good to see Mark. I know this doesn't really make any sense. I had no visible, miraculous signs of any kind, but I know that somehow and, in some way, I saw Mark. My mom asked what I meant by that.

The only way I could answer her was that I didn't see him with my physical eyes, but I saw him with the eyes of my heart. I saw him with my true soul. It's as if God gave me His eyes to see Mark. Perhaps the miraculous "sign" is not something visible but rather something internal. Perhaps the miraculous sign is the fact that I can call this place amazing beauty. This is where Mark met *Jesus* face to face. How much more amazing can you get? This place, where from an earthly perspective a nightmare happened, was transformed into a place where ultimate victory prevailed.

Ultimate evil (Mark's temporary earthly death) happened here. But ultimate good prevailed; Mark's everlasting life began. I'm reminded of the cross. What was meant for evil (Jesus's crucifixion on the cross) was transformed into ultimate good (He saved the world in death). And just like the tragedy of the cross has been transformed into a symbol of ultimate good and victory, I would find out in the coming years how much God does use tragedy for good. He would use my personal tragedy as ultimate good and victory for souls. I would find out how much this would ring true for me as He would reveal to me how Mark's death would change lives.

I have returned to the campground every year now. I only go on June 6. It's interesting how for about four to six weeks leading up to June 6, I am plagued with sadness, anger, and feelings of wanting to quit. But as soon as I make that special pilgrimage to the campground, I am strengthened, refreshed, and put at peace. Once the actual day gets here, I am golden and good to go. I have continued to go up the day before to celebrate, relax, and reflect. I always take a trusted friend and I always "see" Mark every year. In fact, when I start out on my way, I even say out loud, "I'm coming, Cubbie." (Yes, that was a nickname.)

I haven't taken the boys with me yet. I trust that when God knows that their little souls can handle it, they will ask to go visit the place where Daddy met Jesus. And when that happens, I'll take them, and I know it will be perfect. Until they are ready, I will continue to venture to my sacred place and welcome my "new year." I now say that New Year's Day for me is June 6. In fact, one of the best things someone can say to me on Mark's death anniversary, is "happy new year." This is when I celebrate making it another year. It's when I celebrate the honor of being Mark Savage's wife and having his children. It's when I celebrate with joy that Mark has reached ultimate status in his real home—the everlasting heavens. And this is when I celebrate God's faithfulness in continuing to walk ahead of me to guide and lead me, His power to walk beside me to give me strength for current moments, and His promise to walk behind me bringing me through to victory.

CHAPTER 11

Good in Tragedy

I think that it is safe to say that everyone at some point questions the goodness and love of God. If God is really a loving God that wants the best for us, then why is there so much suffering in the world? Why do children get cancer and die? Why are there acts of terror? Why are there shootings? Why do the elderly suffer from Alzheimer's or dementia? Why do husbands get killed under campers? I could go on, but you get the idea. A lot of things go on in this world that are filled with pain and suffering, and that leaves us all wondering how a loving God could let this happen.

I am certainly no exception to questioning God's goodness and love for me. If God is for me, loves me, and wants the best for me, then how is taking my husband, the father of my boys, at the ripe age of thirty-six best for me? How is that good? The thing is that it's not good. I will never believe that Mark being killed under that camper is a good thing. Children getting cancer, terrorist attacks, school shootings, etc., are not good. It's all horrible, and there is nothing good about these tragedies. I will never believe anything different. However, I also don't believe that God causes these tragedies. I believe He allows the tragedy so He can use it for good. Again, the tragedy itself is not good, but it can be used for good. We live in a fallen, broken world that is infiltrated by Satan and evil. When sin entered the world, evil entered the world, and until Christ returns and says, "Enough," evil will continue to run rampant.

I didn't see the good in my tragedy for a while. It wasn't until about two years after Mark's death that I truly understood how Mark's death would be used for amazing good. My pastor asked me if I would be willing to be interviewed by him up on the altar. He wanted to ask me questions and just basically talk in front of the congregation about my story. He wanted me to share what God was revealing to me and what He had allowed me to witness along my journey thus far. I wanted to share too, so I agreed.

I did the interview three times because we had three services at the time. It ended up being very therapeutic and healing for me. It felt good to talk about Mark. It felt good to share what God was revealing to me. It ended up being the situation that changed the life of someone who had come to hear me speak. It was about a week after I did the interview. My kids were running around the church sanctuary one night during vacation Bible school. I noticed a young woman in her twenties who kept looking over at me and smiling. I figured she just thought the kids were cute.

She approached me and asked if I was Shannon. I told her yes, and she introduced herself as Adrienne and told me that she heard my interview at the ten thirty service. Adrienne proceeded to tell me about her life—how she grew up and what the situation was with her father and mother. She shared with me that throughout her whole life she never believed that there was a God. She couldn't understand how, if there was a God, He could have let things happen the way that they did in her life. She told me as she listened to me that day up on the altar that first she bawled. She told me about what hit her the hardest about my interview. I shared my angels, going back to the campground, etc., with the congregation. I also shared a dream I had with Mark in it. Although, to this day, I don't believe it was a dream. I believe it was a direct message from God, and He used Mark to deliver it. It was the sharing of my dream that Adrienne said hit her the hardest.

You are curious about my dream, aren't you? Well, it was about three or four months after Mark died. I was consumed with questions such as: "What does it feel like to be where Mark is right now?" "What does it look like to be where he is?" "Why did he have to die now, this way?" So, one night, I dreamed that Mark and I were sitting in our car. He was sitting in the driver's seat, with me in the passenger's seat. I was crying because I knew that he was dead and that he wasn't staying. I asked him through my tears, "What does it feel like to be where you are?"

Mark laid his head back on the headrest and said "Ohhhhh, I am sooooooo free!" He then raised his head and looked directly at me with the brightest, most piercing blue eyes I have ever seen. I can still see them so vividly to this day, when I think of this. In a most commanding voice he said to me, "Don't you ever feel stupid or silly about telling people how to get here ever again, because I know about the other place too."

I then asked him, "Well, why did you die now, and why like this?" Mark never answered me, and that was it. My dream ended. I have no other memories of that dream. It was over.

It doesn't sound like much, I know. However, let me explain how ironic it is for Mark to say to me, "Don't you ever feel stupid or silly about telling people how to get here ever again because I know about the other place too." Mark played bass in the church worship band. I helped in the church nursery, and we attended church, but we weren't very consistent. We had faith but if I'm being honest, it took a back seat. We were what you call very lukewarm with our faith. I mean, life was good. Up until this point, we had never experienced heartache or real tragedy in our lives, and so of course we thought God was good. We never studied His word or shared our faith with people, because, well, quite frankly, we didn't want to appear to be one of those crazy, fanatical, Jesus people.

The irony of Mark saying that statement to me in my dream is this. We were on our way to church. I remember exactly where we were when he said something significant to me. We were only a few driveways down from the church parking lot. Mark said to me that he wished he could be bolder in his faith, but he didn't want to look like one of those stupid or silly, crazy, off their rocker, religious people.

He then proceeded to say that something really bad must have to happen in your life to bring you so close to God. Do you see how crazy this is? First, how ironic that my "something bad" that has brought me so close to God is his death. He basically said in my dream, what he said to me all those years ago. I find it wild that I even have such a vivid recollection of him saying that years ago. It was a year or so into our marriage. It was before kids. It was a conversation that came out of nowhere while driving in the car.

Coincidence? I don't believe so. That conversation took place to prepare me for this dream. I truly believe that was a message directly from God, and He used Mark to deliver it to me. So what's the message exactly? It's simple. I am to tell my story. I am to tell everyone the story of Mark's death and the amazing revelations that God is showing me so that others can come to know who Jesus Christ is. I am to never feel stupid or silly about sharing the gospel of Jesus. I am not to feel stupid about Jesus being the truth so that others will get to be where Mark is now residing and not end up in the "other place."

> For God so loved the world that He gave his one and only son that everyone who believes in Him will not perish but have eternal life. For God did not send his son into the world to condemn the world, but to save the world through Him. (John 3:16–17 NIV)

> That if you confess by your mouth that Jesus is Lord and believe in your heart that God raised him from the dead you will be saved. For it is with your heart that you believe and are justified, and it is with your mouth that you confess and are saved. (Romans 10:9 NIV)

I've given a lot of thought to why Mark didn't answer the question "Why did you have to die now and why this way?" Honestly, I don't think I'm supposed to know the whole picture right now. I may never know the full picture this side of heaven. Think about it. If we knew the answers as to why everything happens, we would have no reason for faith. We wouldn't read about God. We wouldn't pray to Him. We wouldn't develop *why* questions and put forth the real effort to earnestly seek him. We would have no reason to because we would know everything.

He wants us to earnestly seek Him and have conversation with Him through prayer. He wants us to question Him. He wants us to even yell out in anger to Him when we don't understand. And in those angry and confused moments when we do yell out in anger, He wants us to seek out His word, because when we do, He gives us moments that bring us peace and a certain degree of clarity without having to know the whole big picture. It's when we keep running the race even through the most rugged times and stay faithful, trusting and seeking through any storm that He can and will reveal little inklings as to why things happen. We don't have to see the whole plan to gain that peace that transcends all understanding. We can be more blessed when we don't. "Blessed are those who believe without seeing me" (John 20:29 NLT).

So how exactly does all this prove to be good from tragedy? What is the significance of Adrienne in my story? What kind of impact did the sharing of this dream have on her? She said it was this dream that led her to believe that maybe there really is something like a God and some kind of an afterlife. She told me that she never believed that there was a God, based on circumstances of her life, but she now believed there is something. It was a summer evening that night. When I drove home with the boys after Bible school that evening, I had the top off my convertible, music blaring, boys laughing, and I was crying. Crying joyful tears. It's *this*! Adrienne! This is the good that God was doing with Mark's death. He allowed Mark to die so that God could use him in a dream to me, about sharing the truth of Jesus Christ. My heart was full. My heart was at peace. My tears were grateful tears. I didn't need to cry for Mark. He's made it to his forever home.

Now a seed of faith was planted in Adrienne so that she may come to faith in Christ. He used Mark and me to witness to a young girl with no faith who later down the road, did in fact, commit her life to Christ and accept Him as savior. She also got married. I had the privilege of sitting next to her grandmother (who raised her) at the wedding. Adrienne shared with me how her grandmother enjoyed talking with me.

I only made small talk with her grandmother. Nothing about Mark. But Adrienne talked to her about Mark. She told her about hearing me speak. She told her how Mark died. She told her that hearing me speak was what brought her to faith in Jesus Christ. I was told that for the first time, her grandmother was silent and listened intently to the whole story. Her grandmother, who had been angry about life circumstances, was hearing the good news of Jesus Christ for herself.

So don't you see it? If Mark hadn't died, I wouldn't have shared, Adrienne wouldn't have accepted Christ, Adrienne wouldn't have shared, and her grandmother wouldn't have heard about the love of God. It's like Mark died for Adrienne and her family to learn about the gospel of Jesus. It's weird how Mark's death is so intertwined with this family. It's crazy and beautiful. It's all God at work.

This is what it's all about. Mark is where we all long to be. He is safe. He is beyond happy. He is complete and perfect, lacking nothing. If Mark's death can help point others to Jesus, so that they too will one day be lacking nothing, then I say my tragedy is being used for good. It's better than it would be for him to still be living this earthly life, which is temporary and fleeting to begin with. The afterlife is not.

Adrienne is so special to me. We have a connection like no other. No words can express how much I love and adore her. Although I have told her, I don't believe even Adrienne herself understands the depth of how much she means to me. She is living, breathing proof that Mark did not die in vain. She is a constant reminder of God using Mark's death to bring others closer to Him. She is a beautiful soul whose heart was opened to the love of God through the worst tragedy of my life. She is the beauty that came from my dark, burning ashes.

I can only hope there are others that I may not know about. I really have no way to back this up except for what God has placed in my heart, but I know Mark knows Adrienne and her family. He never knew her when he was alive. But I *know* he knows her now, and one day he'll meet her face to face. He will meet her face to face because he died in his earthly life first and told me he knows about the other place too. He will know her face to face because I shared my story. He will know her face to face because she opened her heart to believe, and, most importantly, Mark will meet her face to face because Jesus Christ died first on that cross, all because He loves Adrienne, He loves Mark, and He loves all mankind. All we must do is be open, be brave, and never feel stupid or silly to share our stories. The only thing left to do is to choose to believe and then receive.

CHAPTER 12

Mark's Legacy

When I think back to the calling hours at the funeral home, I'm amazed at the swarms of people who came through. Calling hours were supposed to be from four to eight in the evening. I stood there greeting people well after midnight. They kept coming. People told me that the line was wrapped down the street and around adjacent buildings, and that there were easily three more hours' worth of people waiting in line.

I can remember looking out across the funeral room, and there wasn't a vacant space. So many people sitting and talking, watching the video of Mark, looking at pictures. I could see people laughing. I assumed there were stories about Mark being shared. I saw many tears being shed as all these people remembered Mark and the role he played in their lives. So many people! So many people I didn't even know. So many people from all different phases of his life. I remember thinking, *How in the world did Mark know so many people?* As I stood there, greeting person after person, I smiled at the stories they would tell me. Everyone had these amazing memories to share with me about how Mark impacted their life for the good. I never felt so proud to be Mark Savage's wife. I never felt prouder to be the woman that gave birth to his sons. I simply was in awe, and I beamed. I was beyond grateful that no other woman would ever have those privileges. They were my privileges and mine alone. No one could ever take that away from me, and my heart was full!

Sometime later—months later after the funeral—Zane came across all the cards and letters that I had received after Mark died. I had stuffed them in a desk drawer; I'm talking thousands of cards and letters. He also found the guest book that everyone signed at the funeral home. He was curious as to what all the cards were and what the book was. So I told him. He flipped through page after page of that filled-up guest book and said, "Wow! A lot of people must have really loved Daddy!" Zane wanted to count how many signatures there were, so that is what we did. We counted and read every name aloud. All 1,022 names!

This took me back to all those people and their amazing stories of Mark. So many people loved him and respected him. It made me wonder what it was about Mark that made people love him so much! How was he able to have so many people that continued to adore him throughout so many phases of his life? He kept up friendships from high school, from college, and from parts of his life that he had moved on from. So many friendships from past phases remained intact up until he died. What was it about him that people loved that made them want to stay in touch with him?

The man was ridiculously intelligent with an off the charts IQ. He was motivated. He was goal driven. He was a hard worker. He was a go-getter, and he was determined to be successful in his professional career. And successful he was. He was an incredibly talented attorney at a top law firm. He was constantly "moving up the ladder," constantly learning, improving himself, and bettering his lawyering skills. His boss had big plans for him. His colleagues had great respect for him. He was admired by many, and there seemed to never be a bad word spoken about him.

Not only was the man ridiculously intelligent, but he was also ridiculously funny, outgoing, and social—so much so that I used to get mad at him because I thought he was flirting with everybody. You could meet Mark, and within five minutes you would have a new best friend. It was impossible to be with him and not laugh. It was impossible to be around him and not feel valued. It was impossible to leave him and not anticipate the next time you would get to hang out with him. He was infectious. He was loyal. He was everyone's best friend.

When I think about why everyone admired, respected, and loved Mark so much, I have concluded it's because he was truly a rare find. He was that rare find of true balance. He was so highly intelligent, but he also had exceptional social skills. Usually the two don't go hand in hand, but with Mark they did. This man, with his professional demeanor, would put on his suit, get up in court, and win court cases. This is the same man, with his Pooh Bear face, who would use a bungee cord to blast two-liter soda pop bottles filled with soda pop through the air because he thought it was great to watch them explode.

He knew how to balance his professional life, without it becoming the end-all. He was a true professional while being down to earth and ridiculously hilarious. I think people loved him because as much as he regarded his education, his success in his professional world, and improving his career, his relationships with people, his kindness toward others, and being a genuine person who thought of others before himself, were all held in higher regard. Mark was always thinking of others. He would stop what he was doing to help anybody out. He would help those who were less fortunate than him. He always credited those to whom credit was due. This was true in both his professional and personal life. He never liked being the center of attention and avoided bragging or being bragged about. He was humble and never sought attention to inflate his ego. Mark loved and treated people with kindness.

I learned a lot of things about Mark after he died. So many stories were shared with me—amazing stories of how awesome my husband really was. One of the most amazing things I learned about was the Starbucks gift cards story. Mark's law office was located on the forty-fourth floor of the Key Tower in downtown Cleveland. He would always go to the Starbucks located in the lobby of that building. Someone had shared with me that Mark used to buy Starbucks gift cards and pass them out to homeless people as he walked across the public square. He said that they deserved to get something warm to eat or drink. I never knew he did that. He never shared that with me.

Mark truly understood what Matthew 6:1–2 is all about: "Be careful not to practice your righteousness in front of others to be seen by them. If you do, you will have no reward from your Father in heaven. So when you give to the needy, do not announce it with trumpets, as the hypocrites do in the synagogues and on the streets to be honored by others" (NIV). Mark knew he didn't have to brag about his good deeds. He just did them. He did them quietly, humbly, and in secret. He did them genuinely. I mean, how genuine is it if you must announce your good deed out loud to others on social media or in person? What's the true intent of your heart if you do so? Are you really wanting to help others, or do you want other people to see how great you are? Mark got this. He didn't need any validation from others. He was confident in himself. His heart was sincere, and he understood that God was the only one he needed validation from. If we are being honest with ourselves, we would admit that we have all fallen into the trap of wanting our good deeds and acts of kindness recognized. I know that I certainly have. After reflecting on Mark's Starbuck's gift card story, I now pay much closer attention to the true intent of my heart. I want to live out Matthew 6:1-2 authentically like Mark did. I want my kindness towards others to be sincere and not for me to gain a pat on the back. I love that this story was shared with me. I still can't believe he never told me that he did that. I love that he didn't.

There are many aspects to the legacy of Mark Savage, but the biggest and by far the best one, is his living legacy who go by the names Zane and Xavier. Those two boys are Mark's most treasured, most amazing, and most brilliant accomplishments. Someone who recognized that was Mark's boss. Mark's boss would come out to my house during those first couple of years after Mark died. I thought it was an amazing thing for him to do. He was the bigwig, and he cared enough to keep in touch and schedule time to see Mark's family. I think it showed how much respect and admiration he had for Mark. He had big plans for Mark that obviously never were brought to fruition.

Mark reciprocated that respect and admiration for his boss. I always heard wonderful things about him, and it really meant a lot to me for him to come see us. He did one of the most amazing things for Zane and Xavier. For me too, but even more so for them. On one of his visits, he brought a gift. He had compiled a bound book of Mark's accomplishments as an attorney. This busy man took the time to go back over Mark's career with him and assemble it all into a book. He brought three copies—one for each boy and one for me. He said that as the boys grow up and find out who they are, he figured that they would really want to know what their father did for a career. He said he tried to keep their friendship relationship out of it and concentrate just on the professional relationship.

He wanted them to know details of what it meant to say, "My dad was an attorney." The book is filled with all the highlights of Mark's time as a lawyer from that law firm. It's filled with the amazing accomplishments of such a talented, young, and promising lawyer. An interview that his boss did is included, as it reveals him talking about Mark being the one to take the reins on so many things and that he was just along for the ride and learning so much from this young up-and-coming lawyer. Of course, the impeccable integrity and phenomenal character that was evident in how Mark treated people was throughout the whole book. And the impeccable integrity and phenomenal character of Mark's boss can't be denied, as this gesture of doing this for Mark's boys reveals. As I read it, I cried like a baby, of course. The boys have not read it yet. They aren't there yet. But what an awesome guide for them as they grow older and start exploring career opportunities. They will learn work ethic, professionalism, and integrity from their father after all. All thanks to Mark's boss.

> Finally, brothers and sisters, whatever is true, whatever is noble, whatever is right, whatever is pure, whatever is lovely, whatever is admirable—if

anything is excellent or praiseworthy—think about
such things. (Philippians 4:8 NIV)

When I stop and think about Mark and everything about him, I
can't help but experience a little rise in frustration and anger. He is
such a huge loss. He is such a huge loss for everyone who knew him.
He is such a huge loss for everyone who didn't get to meet him.
And mostly, it is such a huge loss for me and his boys who have no
choice but to do this earthly life without him. I know where Mark
is, and I know in the depths of my soul that he is more alive now
than he ever was or could be on this earth. And I know that when I
dig down deep, I would not want to take him away from where he
now resides. But I must be honest and tell you that my humanness
sometimes screams, *"Yes, I do want to bring him back to this earth! I
want him with us!"* I think people would be lying if they didn't say
they want that sometimes.

However, things are what they are, and I know that's impossible
to do, so I try to do the next best thing. I create traditions and
events that honor Mark. The boys and I do things that keep his
memory alive. We obviously talk about him all the time. We don't
dwell on him, but we are never afraid to talk about him. The boys
love to hear stories of their dad, and when opportunities present
themselves, I share stories. It's never sad. It's never tabooed to talk
about him. It's done with laughter, smiles, and with great love.

I had Mark's shirts made into quilts. They are called the "daddy
blankets," and they are used all the time. The first Father's Day
after Mark died (it was only a couple of weeks after the accident)
we planted a tree in the backyard. It's our "daddy tree." We tied
red heart helium balloons to it and then launched them to heaven.

We launch balloons every Father's Day. It's amazing to see how big our daddy tree is now. It was such a small little sprig when it was planted. Almost a decade later, it's huge—just as tall as the trees that were already in the backyard. It reminds me how life does somehow go on and so does the love and memories we have for Mark. It grows just as we grow, as we keep walking along our journey.

Another tradition that started was having a birthday party for Daddy. Mark was killed in June. His birthday is in August. I found myself that first year remembering something Mark had said about six months before he died. I remember him standing outside, and for whatever reason he said to me, "Ya know, if anything ever happens to me, I'm going to be really mad at you if you're sitting around all sad and crying. You better have a big party where everyone is eating, drinking, laughing, and having a good time." Isn't it funny he told me that? I truly believe that was the work of the Holy Spirit through Mark. I needed to know that. God knew He was taking Mark home to heaven, and He was preparing me for what I needed to do.

So that first year we had a big party out at the airport hangar where Mark owned a private plane with his best friend. He had a private pilot's license and loved to fly. He enjoyed it so much that he got involved with a charity called Angel Flight, which is an organization that called on Mark to fly patients who needed specific medical care to specific places. (We even named our pug that we got a couple of months after Mark died Angel, in honor of Mark volunteering for Angel Flight.)

That first year, we had around one hundred people at the party. Mark's copilot and best friend was the one who really put it all together. It was sad, no doubt. It was only a couple of months since he died, but it was also the perfect thing to do. So many people gathered to eat, drink, share stories, and, yes, even cry. It rained, but after the rain, we not only got one rainbow, but we got two! Zane spotted them first. As I watched everyone looking at the double rainbow, I saw tears in everyone's eyes and smiles on everyone's lips.

At one point I had a one-on-one conversation with someone about Mark and about Jesus. We talked about how Mark is truly safe in His arms and how *He* really will make everything okay. At one point in this conversation, the sun peeked out over the clouds so intensely that I could barely see even with sunglasses on. I even shielded my eyes and commented on how insanely bright it was. It was so intense that I couldn't see at all. My eyes burned every time I tried to look up. It sounds a bit crazy to say, but it was almost supernaturally bright.

It was as if Jesus was right there with Mark beside Him. I was reminded of Exodus 33:20 NIV: "But he said, you cannot see my face, for no one shall see me and live." It was as if He really was right there. Jesus was there with Mark beside Him, letting me know I'm not alone. I couldn't see Him with my physical eyes because I must still be alive on this earth, but Mark surely was seeing Him, since he now resided in heaven. I knew Mark was there because God allowed him to be. I believe God let Mark know that I was having a birthday party for him. I also felt certain that Mark was proud of me for remembering what he told me about having a party. More importantly, I knew Christ was there, and it was well with my soul.

We continued with the parties out at the hangar for the next several years. The number of guests dwindled, which I figured would happen. It became a party for the most important people who loved Mark the most. All were still invited, but those who cared the most about Mark and for me and the boys were the ones that continued to come. The party went by the wayside the last two or three years for reasons unknown. As time went on, I think we just moved forward, and the party got left behind. We, however, brought the party back this past August, as requested by my youngest, Xavier. It felt right to do, and we are hoping to keep up with it.

Yes, Mark is a huge loss. It will continue to be a huge loss. As my boys get older and change, I anticipate meltdowns and questions as to why Daddy had to die. Because Zane was five and Xavier only two when Mark died, I often think they don't miss what they never knew. I couldn't be more wrong.

My boys feel a void that I can never really relate to. All I can do is support them, allow them to feel whatever emotions come over them, and continue to keep Mark's memory and legacy alive. All I can do is trust that God will provide who my boys need when they need them. All I can do is remind my boys that they do in fact have a father. An amazing father who now lives in heaven. All I can do is remind them that because of Jesus's death on the cross, and because of Daddy's decision to believe in Jesus, he now walks with Jesus every day. It is because of Jesus who intercedes for us that we can ask Him to hug Mark and tell him it's from us.

I will remind them that their daddy loved them on earth and continues to love them from heaven. Even more importantly than that, Zane and Xavier will understand that they have the love of their heavenly Father, who loves them more than any human being could ever love them. Because of that great love, I hope to encourage their faith that God does indeed use every situation (good and bad) to mold us, to grow us and to make us into the people He intends for us to be. It won't always be easy. It won't always feel good. In fact, a lot of the time, it will feel downright unfair and cruel, but when God shows up and reveals pieces of His plan, I pray for the souls of Zane and Xavier to be opened and receiving. I will then be confident that all will be well with their little souls as well.

CHAPTER 13

The Pit of Panic and Anxiety

When Mark died, my life was literally divided into two parts: before Mark's death and after Mark's death. So naturally, New Year's Day for me became June 6. It has become my very own personal New Year's Day when I celebrate making it through another year without Mark. I can honestly say that June 6, 2018, to June 6, 2019, has been the year that I literally didn't think I was going to live through. This was the year that Mark's death—the trauma of the accident—came back and bit me in the butt with a vengeance. Pain that was embedded down deep resurfaced. Fear, irrational thoughts, doubt, loneliness, overwhelmingness, depression, and the most debilitating anxiety and panic attacks struck me.

When I say anxiety and panic attacks, I mean it was a *true* panic disorder. I'm not talking about a little bit of worry over this or that, that would go away once the trigger was eliminated. I'm talking true panic where there were no triggers. It wouldn't subside. My body would be in a constant state of fight-or-flight, sometimes for days, and *nothing* would calm me down. I was downright debilitated and nonfunctional. In my forty-eight years of life, I have never, ever experienced this, and it threw me for a loop. Especially since I am naturally a very go with the flow, easy going, don't sweat the small stuff sort of person. It was truly a living nightmare that I wouldn't wish on anyone. Because panic attacks were a foreign concept to me, I honestly had no idea what was wrong with me, and I didn't think I would survive.

It was late June/early July of 2018 when my deep pit really started. It was shortly after the eighth anniversary of Mark's death. I started to recognize that I was feeling quite depressed. When I get depressed—down and out—I will often isolate myself. Then I get angry that no one checks on me. Which is so dumb. If no one knows anything is wrong, how can they check on you, right? But this is when I started questioning who my true friends were. I was becoming increasingly angry over friends who let me down, friends that I reached out to and who just dismissed me, friends I felt judged by and shamed by when I would open up with my true feelings. I started feeling very overwhelmed with life and felt incredibly alone in my journey. I became increasingly angry over the fact that Mark died. For the first time, I recognized that I may benefit from seeing a counselor. I had never gone to any kind of counseling since Mark died, which is crazy if you think about it. How does one survive what I survived and not go to counseling?

In August I had a routine chiropractor appointment. They took my blood pressure, and it was 160/95. I have never had high blood pressure. It's never over 120/80. I know now that it was a false read. It was taken by a wrist monitor, and it took the woman fifteen minutes to get the thing to work right. I have been told by numerous medical professionals since then that the wrist monitors are super inaccurate. So anyway, it completely scared me to the point that I couldn't let it go. At that time, I didn't know it wasn't accurate. I started having thoughts of what was wrong with me. Suddenly, I became insanely obsessed with the thought of what the boys would do if I died. I'm all they have. There can't be anything wrong with me. As time went by, this thought overtook my brain.

After the birth of my boys, I suffered from postpartum depression. I was put on medication to help with this, and it worked wonders for me. As time went on, I was weaned off that medication; however, this little setback known as "my husband being killed," caused me to have to start that medication again. And again, it was helpful. At the time of this blood pressure episode, I had not been on any medication for depression for eight months or so. I had started working out with personal trainers, changed my eating habits, and had lost thirty pounds. I was feeling so good.

I felt strong physically and mentally, and I felt as if I no longer needed the help of medication, so I stopped and did perfectly fine for eight months. Until the summer of 2018, that is. With depression setting in, feeling overwhelmed and alone, having fears set in and a high blood pressure reading, I felt the need to self-medicate. I started taking my previous medication again without having talked to my doctor.

I had a very bad reaction to it. My body was not the same as it was before when I took it, and it gave me severe side effects. I was advised by the doctors to stop taking it. So I did. And after a few weeks, the side effects subsided, and I felt almost like my normal self. I say almost because I still had irrational thoughts, fear, loneliness, etc., going on. But the physical side effects of self-medicating seemed to be gone, and I thought I was in the clear—that is until November, when I would fall into such a pit that I thought I was going to die.

During September and October, in addition to being obsessed with the thought of the boys being all alone if I die, I became obsessed with finances. I was convinced that all my investments would eventually run out, and I would be homeless someday. I started doubting my decision to quit my teaching job five years earlier. I also became convinced that my boys were not active and healthy enough, so I enrolled us in a boxing class that caused us to run ourselves even more ragged than we already were. I continued to feel alone, overwhelmed, lost, forgotten about, and purposeless.

To top it all off, I also came down with a case of shoulder impingement in my right shoulder. An MRI would later reveal that along with this impingement, I also had two low-grade tears going on in my rotator cuff. I had shoulder therapy for several months, but my ability to do any kind of upper body workout diminished, and I literally couldn't perform normal everyday tasks and self-care skills. It hurt tremendously. I couldn't do even normal life skills with my shoulder, let alone weightlifting.

Suddenly, all that physical and mental strength I was feeling only months earlier was slowing decreasing until it reached the point that it no longer existed. I was put on prednisone in November to help with the inflammation that was going on in my shoulder. This is the time when life became completely unbearable.

In November 2018, the need for a counselor was still recognized. I sought out a therapist and started seeing her once a week. I debated whether to go to a Christian counselor or a secular one. I opted for secular because I needed to deal with Mark's death in a clinical sense. I needed to learn and understand the science behind what happens to one's brain when he or she goes through something traumatic.

I'm not saying that a Christian counselor doesn't do these things, but I felt very strongly that going to a secular counselor was what God wanted me to do. I didn't need to go to someone to hash out my faith. I know what my faith is. I know in the depths of my soul what God's promises are. What I didn't know were coping skills and strategies to deal with my trauma, my anger, my crazy thoughts, and my depression. I don't doubt for a second that I made the right choice. My counselor helped me so much, and to this day, her words ring in my ears when I need to work through episodes of panic and anxiety. I can't say that things got easier or better right away. In fact, things got downright brutal, ugly, and debilitating. When I first started seeing her, I had no idea that I would become so well acquainted with the beasts known as panic and anxiety.

It was right around the same time that I started seeing my counselor that I was prescribed prednisone for the inflammation that was overtaking my shoulder. If you are familiar with prednisone, you know it is a steroid that treats inflammation wonderfully; however, the side effects are not so wonderful. In fact, prednisone will forever be known as the devil to me. I was put on a high dose, and as I was nearing the end of my prescription, I began suffering tremendous side effects that were not common.

I started to notice that as soon as I would pop a prednisone, I would feel weird side effects such as dizziness, a feeling of floating above myself and panic. I didn't want to take them anymore, so when I called the doctor to say what was going on, I was advised to go to the ER to have my heart and blood work checked because what I was experiencing was far from the common and normal side effects. I did eventually check out stable in the ER, and I was told I could skip my last two doses. I needed to be patient and let the medication work its way out of my system. But when time went by, and it finally was out of my system, I didn't feel any better. In fact, I was worse. This is where things get confusing and complicated and horrible.

During the next three months, my body would experience insane physical symptoms that I would understand much later to all be psychosomatic. My mind would endure agonizing distress with such agonizing thoughts that I thought for sure the only help for me would be to have me committed to a psych hospital. I literally thought I was going crazy, and life as I knew it was over. The irrational thoughts of being overwhelmed, being alone, fearing something was wrong with me, fears over what would happen to my boys if I died too, feelings of being a failure, financial worries to the point I was convinced I would be homeless, (and the list goes on and on) were magnified by 100 percent. When I reflect on November through January, it is unbelievable the physical ailments my body went through. It seemed that one ailment would present itself, run its course, and then another ailment would appear that was just as horrible if not worse than the previous one.

In the beginning it started with profuse sweating. So much sweating that I would have to change shirts three times in the middle of the night. I had intense shivering and chills with uncontrollable shaking, although my skin was hot to the touch. I had tingling throughout my entire body. It felt as if I was being pricked everywhere with pins and needles. Every day, different muscles and joints would ache so much that I could barely walk. My legs would shake and feel as if they would give out.

At one point I was convinced that I had too much neck adjustment at the chiropractor and that my neck was permanently damaged and would crack in half. I couldn't walk up the stairs without being completely out of breath and needing to lie across my bed to gain composure. My heart raced and palpitated. My chest was tight, and I was convinced I had heart issues. I also thought I was having a stroke at one point. I admitted myself to the ER because I was convinced of it. I wasn't. I had CAT scans and even saw a cardiologist who had me wear a heart monitor for two weeks.

All results revealed that I was not anywhere close to having a stroke, and nothing was wrong with my heart. I was so confused. I was feeling all these ailments, but there was never anything medically wrong with me. At this point I did not understand that I was experiencing panic attacks.

Sleeping became nonexistent. I would try to close my eyes, and just when I would start to fall asleep, I would awaken to what felt like electric shock throughout my body. The only way to describe it is that it felt like my body was jumping out of itself, and my heart could not catch it. This electric shock was so intense that my little dogs, who would sleep up against my body, would jump away from me.

It felt as if I was literally crawling out of my skin, but I couldn't go anywhere. I couldn't stop it. When I would be jolted like this, my mind struggled with remembering who I even was and where I was. I couldn't even remember who my kids were. I knew I had them but couldn't remember who they were or where they were. For weeks on end, I had many nights with minimal sleep.

It was so bad that I would get my will out and lay it on the dining room table because I was certain that I was going to die on my couch and not see the morning. I would write my cell phone passcode down so that the boys would be able to get into my contacts once they found me dead. I was surely wrestling with the devil, and I was certain he was going to win.

I feared the night and getting ready for bed because I knew what I was up against. I anticipated it and every night my anticipation of the devil showing back up to have another wrestling match always seemed to become my reality. When I would close my eyes, I would literally see demons in my mind's eye gnashing their teeth, which would instantly cause me to open my eyes.

On those rare nights when I managed to fall asleep for an hour or two, I would fear waking up in the morning because I would instantly be plagued with intense nervousness in my stomach. It was like a knotted rope in the pit of my stomach, all tangled and intertwined with my organs, squeezing them. This sensation would rise and rise until I could not lie there anymore. I could no longer lounge because the heaviness in my stomach wouldn't allow me to do so. I would wake up and anticipate the continued nightmare I was living. I wanted to feel normal, and I wanted it so desperately. I never got my normalcy.

I had severe dizziness, tunnel vision, lightheadedness, and shaking. I would walk around feeling as if I was floating above myself. Have you ever been drunk, and you try to play it off like you're not, but no matter how hard you try to play it off, it's obvious that you are? Well, that's what I felt like. That's the best way to describe it. I would get intense rushes of hot adrenaline through my body. I could feel it from head to toe. The palms of my hands would develop deep tenderness, itching, numbness, and superhot, burning sensations.

The only way to have an ounce of relief from them was to wrap them in ice. I would get the same hotness and numbness in my ankles and feet but not as intense as in my hands. I became obsessed with Googling all my "symptoms" and I was convinced I had peripheral neuropathy. I also became convinced that I had severe nerve damage throughout my entire nervous system. It felt as if someone was squeezing my forearms with a vice-like grip, compressing them until they would break. I had deep pains in my calves, and my legs were cracking.

When I would drive, I would feel shooting pains down my shoulders, into my arms, my neck, my back, and my legs. My entire body was cracking and breaking apart. All my nerves were being pinched and damaged, and I was positive that the shoulder impingement in my right shoulder was the cause of all of this.

I was nauseous and had no appetite. At times I would gag and throw up even with the smallest bits of food. I had intense thirst. I couldn't get enough water. At times I would drink water so fiercely that I couldn't catch my breath. I had many moments of restlessness where I would pace the floor. I would lose all focus at times so badly that I couldn't even formulate words. Any little mark that would appear on my body somewhere was surely a symptom of some disease. I ended up getting a little burn on my arm from my curling iron. I had no recollection of doing that, and I was certain that this mark was an indication of cancer.

I was deathly afraid to be alone, and so my mom, my sister, and one of my dearest friends would spend the night with me. I began taking walks around the neighborhood at ten o'clock at night to try to calm myself down, and I couldn't even walk normally. I would stumble over my feet and had to be consciously aware of how I was stepping. I would get so mad and scream at myself, "Walk like a normal person!" The only places I could go to get even an ounce of reprieve was my shower or my hot tub.

As I would find out through my counseling, everything physical I was experiencing was due to anxiety, panic, and fight-or-flight mode. I was experiencing intense anxiety and panic attacks. I would find out that anxiety and panic manifest in real physical symptoms that leave you convinced that there is something horribly medically wrong with you. I would find out that fight-or-flight mode is a real response that a person's body will go into when in danger and wanting to flee. This is what I was experiencing, except I was never in real danger and never really needed to flee.

Everything I was experiencing was truly psychosomatic, and I would be stuck in a state of pure panic and fight-or-flight for sometimes days on end. I wasn't just a little worried or concerned about something; I was in a deep, dark, nasty pit with a real disorder, and it struck me down hard. It was a living nightmare of full-blown irrational fear and panic. It's insane to me how the physical ailments that manifest with panic disorder are only a figment of the imagination. However, at the same time, it's very, very real.

The brain is a crazy thing. It's wild how it can trick your whole body into experiencing such physical agony. I was in a constant state of this for basically three straight months with very little release from it. Not many people knew what I was enduring. I masked it well. To look at me during that time, you would never guess that I was in that state.

I looked calm and happy. I would put on a smile and laugh and carry on a conversation if I needed to. No, you would never guess where I really was. However, I can assure you that I was anything but calm and happy. I was in chaos. I'm pretty sure my mother had thought I lost my mind. My dad would hug me and tell me to let it out. I would cry on him and through my sobs say that all I wanted was to be happy with my kids, and I can't get there.

I didn't know what was wrong with me. All I knew was that Satan was having a field day with me, and I was certain that he was slowly killing me. The reality, though, is that Satan wasn't killing me. He may have been trying to, but I belong to Christ, and, well, we all know Christ trumps Satan. I would soon experience relief from my anxiety and panic attacks through intense therapy and medication. I would also experience the restoration of my soul that I had been praying so desperately for over the last three months. This restoration would come in the forms of therapy, medication, and, most importantly and most securely, Jesus's anxiety.

CHAPTER 14

Therapy, Medication, and Jesus's Anxiety

I never considered myself someone who needed professional counseling. Surely I was strong enough to maneuver my way through things by myself. I always thought I wasn't crazy enough to need therapy. Isn't that who therapy is for? Crazy people? I certainly wasn't crazy. I hesitated to go to a counselor because, honestly, I always viewed it as nonsense and felt that it really wouldn't do anything. Plus, I figured if I was going to need counseling, I would have needed it back when Mark first died, not almost a decade later.

Was I ever wrong, about everything. I discovered that there is a little bit of cray-cray in all of us, including me. I learned that therapy is not nonsense but is the exact opposite and is vital to my emotional health and overall well-being. I came to understand that the need for professional counseling has no timeline or time frame.

When I first started counseling sessions, I was suddenly feeling completely overwhelmed with my life. Suddenly, I had irrational fears and thoughts. I felt incredibly alone and a complete failure. For the first time since Mark's death, I felt incredibly weak mentally and tremendously worrisome.

I was very angry about the desertion of "friends," and I wanted to quit. I wanted to quit this life. I felt 100 percent stuck with no way out, and this is how it would forever be. Things got a whole lot worse in my counseling sessions before they got better. I believe this happened for a few reasons. First, things were being dredged up. Pain was coming to the forefront, and I was getting real with my emotions for the first time in a long time. I was beginning to admit to things, which I hadn't done since Mark died.

Second, I started taking medication halfway through my therapy experience. I was deathly afraid of antidepressants/anxiety medications, and I vowed to kick whatever this was to the curb naturally. However, I was struck with such severe anxiety/panic that my body could not stabilize without it.

Third, the prednisone I was taking for my shoulder issues was kicking into high gear. I believe the prednisone had a lot to do with the severe anxiety and panic attacks that wrecked my life. I don't know if it was necessarily the cause of the panic disorder that manifested, but I know it didn't help.

First things first. What did I uncover during my therapy sessions? Well, for starters I learned that I was awfully hard on myself. I learned that I was doing the best I could with my life and that my best was pretty good. In fact, I discovered that even my worst was better than most who were raising kids in a two-parent household. I acknowledged that the boys and I have experienced a tremendous loss. Mark's death is a *huge* blow, and we did get robbed. I discovered that anytime I would feel weak, I would shove it down into a hole and say to myself, "Stay strong, Shannon. Stay strong." I believed that if I didn't stay strong and handle everything by myself that I would be viewed as weak. I was constantly being told how strong I was. How much of an inspiration I was. I had taken on the mentality that if I break, then I'm letting people down. I wouldn't be an inspiration or an encouragement to others.

I had it in my mind that I had been dealt this horrible situation, and I was going to prove to the world that it wasn't going to stop me or bring me to my knees. I was going to thrive throughout this, and breaking was not an option in thriving. The thing is that I learned that in order to thrive, I had to break. And breaking is what I officially did, and it never felt better! Well, not at the time did it, but in retrospect, yes.

I finally admitted that I was fearful of being alone. I was afraid that I would die alone with no one to care for me. I acknowledged and mourned the life that was taken from me. I admitted that, yes, I still want Mark here in my life. And that it was okay to wish that and to admit that. I always thought that if I admitted that I wish I could still have Mark, that meant I would never be ready to move on and welcome new love into my life, which to this day, I pray is part of God's plan for my future.

However, I can't move forward without truly acknowledging what was taken from me. I discovered that God does not sit on His throne expecting me to be happy and accepting of what has happened in my life. In fact, I believe He welcomes my cries of anger, sadness, and frustration. I would truly shove my emotions down in fear that I would disappoint God for being angry and not trusting Him with His plan for my life. Basically, I was afraid I would be a Christian hypocrite by not accepting Mark's death without any questions asked. I did more damage to myself by not allowing myself to be real with God.

I now believe that God wants me to cry out to Him with all these emotions. I now believe this does not make me a hypocrite but makes me very real. I believe that God wants me to get angry and question because when I do, it is then that I want to understand. So it leads me to dive into His word, seeking answers, seeking understanding, and seeking comfort. And I will get it. Not completely, but I will get enough that it brings forth healing.

It is during our worst times that we find Him and want Him. And that's what He ultimately wants. He wants us to draw closer, to learn about Him and His ways. That's what our human emotions prompt us to do. So I embraced my human feelings and allowed myself to cry like a toddler at Mark's grave site again, grieve for Mark again, be angry again, and ultimately seek Him again.

I have this wine rack at home. Written across the front of it are words such as *smile, laugh, play, dance, party, celebrate,* and *love.* That piece of furniture was brought into my home because those words screamed *me.* Even after Mark's death, those words captured my heart and soul. My spirit embodied those words, and at the time of starting counseling sessions, I lost that spirit. I was lost. I couldn't find me. I couldn't get back to that place. I remember sharing about this piece of furniture with my counselor and telling her that I can't find my way back to that. The woman that lived those inspirational words was gone, and I can't find her.

She assured me that we would find that Shannon again. One of the ways she helped to find that Shannon again was through a therapy called acceptance and commitment. Basically, it was learning to acknowledge and accept that this horrible circumstance happened to me, but I am going to commit to what's most important to me and trudge forward anyway. So she asked me one day what my values are. Not my goals. Goals are set in response to what you value. So she asked me what I valued most. Without much hesitation, I remember answering her with these two things. Number one, my faith in Jesus Christ, and two, my two boys, in that order. I was then presented with the question of what I am doing to commit to those values.

At the time, I wasn't feeling like much of a mother. I didn't think I was doing enough, but in hindsight, the value of being a mother to my boys was always intact. I don't believe there was anything more I could have been doing. I see that now. I did, however, make a real effort to spend quality time with my boys.

But when I thought about the value of my faith, it was a little more difficult. I came to the realization that my passion for sharing my story—my journey since Mark's death—had dwindled. I used to share so much of God's realness on social media. I would be invited to talk in front of groups of people about His realness and my tragedy. I told my counselor that I wanted to write a book. I had so much to share, and I had things written already, but it became stagnant.

She asked me, "Why aren't you doing that, then?"

And so here I am—on fire to write my book. It's been something that I've been prompted to do for a while. It never felt like the right time. Until now. I thought there would be a day that I would officially "be over" the death of my husband and "be over" that traumatic night. I now know that I'll never be over it. The wound will always be open to a certain extent. It can close smaller, but it will always be there.

The trauma of that night will always be there. I needed to understand this. People need to understand this. They need to understand this when dealing with someone who experiences a deep loss due to death, and they need to understand this for themselves, if they ever find themselves in this same kind of situation.

I also believe that God wanted me to experience the severe panic attacks that I did for very specific reasons. What I described in the previous chapter threw me for a loop. I sought out a therapist to talk through unresolved issues about Mark's death, so it was frustrating to me that as the weeks went by, a lot of time was spent in discussing and learning how to cope with panic attacks! I wanted to talk about Mark, and we did, but I was so taken aback and surprised at how therapy progressed. My therapist wasn't though. Along with accepting and committing, discovering my values and uncovering repressed grief and allowing myself to miss Mark, I also was learning about this thing called fight-or-flight response. I already shared in the previous chapter what happened to my body and my mind throughout the panic attacks, so now, I'd like to share about how I learned to cope with it.

I wanted this demon of anxiety and panic to *go away*! I had never experienced something as horrible as these panic attacks in my entire life, and so I just wanted it *gone*! But waking up and just praying for it to not rear its ugly head for the day made it rise and take over. The more I wished it away, the worse it would become. I had to learn how to accept that anxiety and panic attacks, for some reason, were now a part of me. But they aren't the biggest part of me. They are only a small part of Shannon, and I had to learn how to take it for a ride and not let it take me for a ride. I had to learn how to acknowledge when I felt heightened, and how to let it be and choose commitment to my values once again. And honestly, to this day, when I feel a slight rise, I acknowledge it, let it be, and without much time or thought, it's gone.

I was introduced to breathing, mindfulness, and meditation in therapy. So in all my realness and honesty, when my counselor first talked about breathing, I wanted to laugh and quit therapy. I have heard of breathing techniques and meditation before and always thought it was nonsense. However, I was so desperate to feel normal again that I was willing to try. Not just try, but to commit to sticking with it and really giving it a fair shot. I pleasantly found that it helped tremendously, and I fell in love with these practices. Sometimes, I would have to stop my day and go lie on the couch in the basement and "breathe" twenty times a day. I downloaded meditation apps on my phone, and I started to use them regularly. I downloaded both secular apps and Christian meditation apps. I love them both. The Christian apps are centered around prayer and meditating on scripture. I'm a Jesus girl to my core, and so I crave this type of meditation. The secular apps I discovered help me to understand the science behind anxiety and panic; therefore, it provided the necessary calm.

I also discovered that walking outside in nature was a tremendous coping skill for me. All this happened in the winter, so I would bundle up, seek out different parks, and walk. I began to love it. I loved the cold air. I loved the snow. I loved seeing my boot footprints in the snow. I loved the sights in the woods. I loved the silence and the peacefulness. I loved the slight sounds I could hear even amongst the silence. I was learning how to be mindful of the present. When I would feel the rising of a panic episode brewing within me, I would bundle up and hit the outdoors. It helped a lot.

In fact, the cold, snowy weather walks were going to be missed, but spring and summer walking appeared promising.

On one beautiful spring day, I decided to sit in silence in the middle of my town square. It was a gorgeous, sunny, and breezy day. I decided to take out a piece of paper and write down every sound I heard in the town square. It's a busy place with lots of traffic, but who would ever have thought that I would write down thirty-five different sounds! It was a supercool experience. That day, I truly experienced what it meant to be mindful of the present. I was so acutely aware of sounds. There were no thoughts of the past or of the future. I was completely in the present, focused on sound alone. I found it amazing what happened to my soul when I was still, quiet, and mindful, not hurried, or concerned with others.

Despite learning these coping strategies for anxiety and panic attacks, I still struggled with coming out of that intense fight-or-flight mode. When I would practice the walking, the mindfulness, the breathing, and the mediation apps, the relief would be so short-lived. I'm talking just in the moment short-lived. I would practice one of these coping skills but then instantly be back in that horrible state of fight-or-flight, complete with all the physical symptoms I previously described, and the same debilitating thoughts would always resurface.

My therapist suggested medication along with my therapy, but I was convinced that I had to overcome all this naturally. I was deathly afraid of any kind of medicine. I had such a bad reaction to a previous medication that I self-medicated with at the beginning of summer, and the prednisone was the devil to my system (I'll talk more about that in a bit), so I was convinced that all prescribed meds were bad. In fact, I was so petrified of putting any kind of toxin in my body that I wouldn't even drink coffee or have a glass of wine. My irrational thoughts that came along with the anxiety and panic attacks had me convinced that even coffee and wine would do damage to me. I was beyond miserable. Miserable isn't even the word for it.

I could no longer go on like this, so I did finally talk with my primary care physician. As much as I hated to do it at the time, I started taking Zoloft for the intense panic that was a constant in my body. I think my doctor was reaching the point of being fed up with me. She told me that I needed to surrender and trust her that this is what she believed I needed right now. It wasn't easy to do at first. She started me out on a very low dose, and it did make me feel worse before it made me feel better.

But I stuck with it and did what she told me, and eventually my body began to stabilize, and I was starting to feel some relief. I mean real relief, where I would have moments of the real Shannon peek through, and for the first time, I believed there to be light at the end of the tunnel.

I thought giving in and taking an antidepressant/anxiety medication meant I was weak. I wanted to fight all this naturally, and I felt like a failure at first because I couldn't do it without the help of a medication. But here's the thing about antidepressant and anxiety medications. Sometimes, they are needed. I'm not talking about popping a pill for a little bit of sadness or a little bit of worry. I'm talking about when your brain has a true chemical imbalance that causes you to fall into such a pit that you can't even function. When there is a true imbalance of chemicals in your brain, no amount of positive talk or even coping skills can bring you fully out of it.

It's like the analogy of someone with diabetes or high blood pressure. You can't talk your way out of diabetes. You can't talk your way out high blood pressure. The organs that are affected by those conditions are lacking something. You can't fix it without medication. It's not a new analogy. You've probably heard that a hundred times, but it's true, and its true for the brain as well. I don't know if this theory about the brain has been proven, but I firmly believe that when the brain is lacking in chemicals, or off balance in a chemical way, you can't fix it by positive talk. It needs some help.

This is where my brain was, I believe. My brain was suffering from a chemical imbalance. And like with diabetes or high blood pressure, certain people are more prone to it. I think I'm one of those people. I had severe postpartum depression after the births of my sons. I had severe depression after the death of Mark (Who wouldn't, really?), so I think I'm one of those people prone to mental setbacks. And I'm okay with that, because that's how God has wired me.

Speaking of chemical imbalance in the brain, this leads me to my prednisone experience. As I said previously, I was put on prednisone for the inflammation in my shoulder caused by the impingement and tears I had. I suppose it brought down the inflammation, but I believe it did much more damage to my brain and to my body as a whole. I was put on a high dose, and I had side effects of profuse sweating, hotness and tingling to my skin, and the jitters from the get-go. Things got bad after the bulk of the prednisone prescription got into my system. This was when I started to experience the intense anxiety/panic attacks and fight-or-flight mode.

After learning about prednisone from my doctor and my therapist, and researching on my own, I learned that prednisone can have severe side effects that are not normal or common side effects. I learned that prednisone can cause mental side effects such as panic attacks, paranoia and actual psychosis. It can alter neurotransmitters in the brain such as serotonin. As I reflect on the time frame of when I got struck with all that craziness, it falls right into when that medicine kicked into my system. Even though I eventually stopped the medicine, and there seemed to be enough time for it to clear out of my system, I wonder if the damage was already done. I wonder if the prednisone altered the chemicals in my brain so much that my brain no longer could function normally as I knew it. It was as if my brain had now had a taste of what it feels like to experience irrational thoughts, high panic and anxiety—paranoia that it now had to be retrained.

I wanted clear and precise answers as to why—seemingly out of nowhere—I suddenly was experiencing very real and very intense episodes of anxiety and panic. I was convinced it had to be the prednisone. It was a vicious thought cycle: Did the prednisone cause this state of being, or was it the anxiety and panic causing me to think it was the prednisone? I even thought back to the reactions I had to the medicine that I self-medicated with and wondered if the side effects from that weren't really side effects at all but panic attacks, and I didn't know what I was experiencing. I ended up driving myself even crazier by trying to piece everything together and figure it out. It kept going around and around.

I finally learned that all this trying to figure out the cause was increasing the anxiety and panic. It wasn't helping me one bit to be so concentrated on figuring this out. I eventually had to come to terms with that it didn't matter what caused it—it meaning the demons of anxiety/panic attacks. They were now here, and I had to learn to cope with them no matter how or why they emerged.

After some time, my mind and body began to stabilize and I reached the conclusion that it was a combination of things. Things were brewing within me back in the summer. I had feelings and emotions about Mark's death that needed to be addressed. A lot of these feelings were coming up during counseling sessions, and I often felt worse than better after those beginning sessions. I also believe that I really did have horrible effects from being on the prednisone. I do believe that it set things into even higher gear and did indeed set my already overthinking brain into full-blown panic and fear. It was like a perfect storm of horrendous events all coming together at the same time. It all wreaked havoc on my mind, body, and soul. For whatever reason, God was allowing all of this chaos to ensue in my life, and I now had to commit to retraining my brain—change old habits and make new ones—and ultimately trust in Him that He was allowing all of this for a purpose.

My faith in Jesus Christ has taught me that He will never allow me to go through something without purpose. I do believe in the depths of my soul that He uses the horrible for good. I believe He is growing me through hardships. I believe that everything debilitating He allows into my life is ultimately Him wanting me to grow closer to Him with a deeper understanding of who He is.

However, during the peak of my attacks, I honestly could not understand why He was allowing me to go through such a crippling ordeal. I could not fathom that there was anything I could possibly learn about Him by enduring nonstop panic attacks! I recall that one night my girlfriend Paula came over to stay the night because I was deathly afraid to be alone. I was sitting on my front porch when she drove up my driveway. She got out of the car and sat next to me on the porch.

I put my head on her shoulders, and I had tears streaming down my face. I was so incredibly sad. It was like an emotionless sad. *Sad* is the only word I can think of to describe it. I couldn't feel anything. All I could do was cry. It was a hopeless feeling. I felt like a shell of a person whose soul had literally been ripped out. There was nothing inside of me, and all I could do was cry numbing tears.

I remember saying to Paula, "Why, oh why, is He allowing me to go through this? Why is He not taking it away? If He is there, why is He not rescuing me from this?" I said this out loud to Paula, but I was really saying it to God too. I was saying it more to Him than I was to Paula. I had serious doubts that He was listening. I had serious doubts of His existence at that moment. How could He really allow me to experience such a nightmare if He loved me and was there with me? He already took my husband from me. He already forced me into being a solo parent. Wasn't that enough suffering? He turned my world upside down already. Why was He not allowing me to move forward with peace and happiness? At that moment, I was certain that He had no understanding of how horrible this was. He had no idea how hollow and dead I felt inside. He had no idea how out of reach He made Himself to me. That is, in fact, if He was truly there.

A couple of weeks after that night on my porch with Paula, I started to feel better. I was staying faithful to my counseling sessions, the anti-anxiety medication was starting to kick in, and my brain was starting to balance out, to the point that I could finally read again and comprehend it. It was also during these weeks that it became apparent that God heard me that night on my front porch.

Like I said, I could finally focus on a book again, so I reread a book that I had read well over a year ago. One of the chapters focused on intense fear, anxiety, and panic. But not just anyone's intense fear, anxiety, and panic. It was *Jesus's* intense fear, anxiety, and panic. Do you know about the Garden of Gethsemane? This is where Jesus was betrayed by Judas Iscariot and arrested by the Romans to be crucified. This is where Jesus prayed to His Father (God) to please take away the burden of having to be arrested, beaten, and crucified on the cross, yet He submitted to the Father's will anyway. "Father, if you are willing, take this cup from me; yet I want your will to be done, not mine." (Luke 22: 42 NLT). Usually when you see pictures of Jesus praying in the Garden of Gethsemane, it appears that He is praying calmly, in total peace with what was about to happen. But Jesus was anything but calm and peaceful. He was crying out to God to please take this cup away from Him. He didn't want to do it. Scripture tells us that Jesus was so filled with fear and anxiety that He was sweating blood. "And being in anguish, he prayed more earnestly, and his sweat was like drops of blood falling to the ground" (Luke 22:44 NIV). I wondered if you could really be in so much anguish, as scripture called it, to the point of sweating blood. I found out that this is a real medical condition called hematidrosis. It's a real condition where people are in such a high state of anxiety that they can sweat blood from their skin when there is no cut or injury present. It's rare, but it's real, and Jesus experienced this. Jesus, the Savior of the world, had experienced such crazy high anxiety in that garden that night. He knew what was about to happen to him. He knew He was going to die. He knew that there was nothing to stop it. Talk about being in a state of fight-or-flight!

When I realized this for the first time—that Jesus was experiencing panic attacks—I was taken back to that night on my front porch with Paula. I had cried out to God asking Him why He was allowing this. I cried out wondering why Jesus was not rescuing me from it. I didn't believe that night that He could possibly have any understanding of what I was going through. Then a couple of weeks later, God revealed Himself to me in a way I had never thought of before. He revealed to me that, *yes*, He did know what I was going through. He knew it all too well. He knew it even more intensely than I knew it, which I can't even comprehend.

The constant state of being in fight-or-flight truly made me believe that it was going to kill me. I had moments of such high panic attacks that I really felt as if I was going to die. Jesus knew He was going to die. He knew there was no way out of going to the cross. He knew the horrible physical death He was about to endure. I thought and I felt as if I was going to die while having these horrible attacks. But Jesus *knew* He was going to die. Not from the attacks He was experiencing, but for the sins of the world, and there was nothing He could do about it.

At this moment, I now understood what God wanted me to learn about Him. I now understood that God was revealing to me that there is nothing—I mean absolutely nothing—that I can experience on this earth that Jesus didn't experience first. Although He was fully divine, Jesus was sent to earth as fully man to understand and relate to our human thoughts, feelings, temptations, and emotions. And, yes, even being able to relate to intense fight-or-flight mode. He is not excluded from anything I feel or go through.

He experienced it all so that He can pull me through—so He can intercede to the Father on my behalf to lift the cups we have to endure. His cup of being crucified on the cross was not lifted so that our cups can eventually be. I cried out to God that night on my porch asking why He was allowing me to go through this. I get it now. I get it that it was a way for me to identify with Christ and a way for Him to identify with me. It brought yet a deeper understanding and appreciation for the actions at the cross. Appreciation isn't even the word for it. It's more like a forever indebted heart for something I don't deserve. He died for me, and I did nothing for such sacrifice.

When this realization came to me, I heard Him screaming out to me, "Shannon, I've got you girl!" And I believed it wholeheartedly with gratitude and with thankfulness. Gratitude because He was restoring me, and thankfulness that I got to experience such agony, because it only connected me to Him that much more. As hard as it is for me to comprehend, I was only enduring a fraction of the pain and severity during my panic attacks compared to the pain and severity of what Jesus was enduring during His panic attacks that night in the garden. It only deepens my heart for Him. It puts in perspective the reality of what Him going to the cross does for me. He, once again, amazed me with how He uses *everything* to teach me, grow me, and bring me to a deeper connection with Him.

CHAPTER 15

Reflection

I often wonder what my life would be like if Mark hadn't died. How would our marriage be? Would we still be married? Would I still be teaching? Would we still be living in Ohio? How different would the boys be? Would they be happier? Would their personalities, likes, and dislikes be different? Who would I be friends with? Would I be more involved with "cliques" of people because I would be part of a couple?

I truly believe that becoming a widow at the age of thirty-eight, with two little boys to raise, has got to be one of the loneliest and most isolating situations that a woman can find herself in. Being a solo parent from the time that my kids were basically babies (ages two and five), puts me into a category like no other. I call it solo parenting because that is exactly what it is. It's solo. It's not single. Single parenting is the result of a divorce. Solo is the result of a death. I had absolutely *zero* say in my future. I had no choice to exit my marriage. I was left with no decision. It was made for me. It was completely out of my control. My boys have had no choice to get to know their father. Mark had no choice whether to spend time with his boys or not. All these choices or decisions were completely out of our control. See the difference? It's solo parenting. It's not single.

I often feel as if I never fit anywhere. Single friends cannot identify with me. They have never had a true love in marriage, let alone to lose it. Divorced friends cannot relate. I've heard people say that divorce is like a death. *"Like* a death." It's *not* a death, however. I don't argue that it's not painful, I'm sure. And I believe there is mourning after a divorce; however, it's not a death. Again, there was a decision or a choice made with a divorce. I don't believe for a second that the two can be related or compared. I can't fit in with the older widows who have lost their spouses after a lifetime. They raised their kids and even welcomed grandchildren into the world together. It's a totally different kind of widow altogether.

Not even young widows with no kids can relate. The pain you feel for yourself after losing your spouse is overwhelmingly debilitating. But when you have kids, and you can't fix it for them? It downright kills your soul. It was said to me at one point that having kids would probably make it impossible to "get over this." That comment made me wonder if it would be easier if I hadn't had Mark's boys. I wondered if I was forever in deep grief because I would be reminded of Mark every time I looked at the boys.

But that's just it. I am reminded of Mark every time I look at my boys. What an incredible gift. I know that it's the opposite. I would forever be in deep grief if I *didn't* have Mark's living legacies to raise. How unfortunate for those who find themselves without a late spouse's children to raise. In fact, it's because of them that I will trudge forward. It's because of them that Mark lives on. There are support groups for the elderly widowed, the divorced, the single, but not so much for the young widow with kids who was robbed of the life she thought she would have. It's like I was thrust into the worst club that no one chooses to join. You are forced into it, and it's either sink or swim. I can only speak of my personal experience, but it was either sink or swim with very little outreach from others.

I have often felt excluded. I have often felt forgotten about. I have often felt as if people think "I'm over it." In fact, someone even made the statement, "I know he died and everything, but when is she going to get over this?" I've often been told that it's silly to feel those things. But the reality is that unless you have walked in my shoes, you can't tell me how silly it is. No one knows how my youngest son, after nine years since his father died, has a breakdown and asks me why Daddy had to die with tears running down his face. No one gets how I am the only one solely responsible for raising my kids, paying the bills, taking care of the house, and taking care of myself. No one can understand the fear I often feel that I won't make it all right for my boys, and what if they one day wish it were me under the camper instead of their father? No one understands how I live with flashbacks of that night *every single day*! It's not intense like it was when it first happened, but every day I wake up and one of my first thoughts is, "Mark died," and some detail of that night scrolls through my mind.

No one has any idea how infuriating it is when people comment on how windy some storm was that the trees were bending. *Hmm!* That's nothing. I can tell you about wind. No one can even grasp how I, to this day, feel guilty because I lived, and Mark died. No one can possibly understand that such a traumatic event can never ever leave me. All I can do is move forward the best that I can. No one can possibly understand how I had become stricken with severe anxiety and panic attacks almost a decade after Mark's death.

I've written about a lot of things that people will never understand. I'm certain it comes across quite negative and even bitter sounding. It's not that I am bitter or even negative. It's reality. I'm being very real when I say no one understands these things. Only the handful of people who happen to be in my same circumstance can. And even those who are in "the club" can't totally understand because everyone's experience is different. It's not all negative and bitter, though. I have a lot of beyond-beautiful moments that have been brought on because of Mark's death. I have experienced what it truly means to be blessed because of Mark's death. That statement right there is one not many people can understand.

What does it mean for you to be truly blessed? Is it because you have been given a beautiful spouse? Beautiful, happy, and healthy kids? Are you financially stable? Are you in good health? Do you have opportunities for vacations, cars, good jobs? Are you successful in your career? Have you reached a status of power in your professional world? Are you blessed with great family and friends? If I'm being honest, it totally bugs me when people call themselves blessed regarding these things. This does *not* mean I don't find these things all blessings. They absolutely are. They are all things to be grateful for. Things to desire and things to strive for. Don't misunderstand me when I say I'm bothered by it when people say they are blessed with these things. They are absolutely blessings. However, here's my but. They are all blessings *but*, what if they were all taken from you? What if you get sick? What if you lose your job? What if your husband is killed under a camper and your world as you know it comes crashing down, and there is no fixing it? Would you still call yourself blessed? Jesus says you are. Are you familiar with the beatitudes listed by Jesus in the Sermon on the Mount?

> Blessed are the poor in spirit, for theirs is the kingdom of heaven. Blessed are those who mourn, for they will be comforted. Blessed are the meek, for they will inherit the earth. Blessed are those who hunger and thirst for righteousness, for they will be filled. Blessed are the merciful, for they will be shown mercy. Blessed are the pure in heart, for they will see God. Blessed are the peacemakers, for they will be called children of God. Blessed are those who are persecuted because of righteousness, for theirs is the kingdom of heaven. Blessed are you when people insult you, persecute you and falsely say all kinds of evil against you because of me. (Matthew 5:3–11 NIV)

Okay, so wait a minute. Isn't the meaning of the word *beatitude* blessedness? Wouldn't that mean a beatitude is something good, something happy, something that brings you joy? When I Google synonyms for the word *beatitude*, I find words like *bliss, happiness, peace,* and *serenity.* Jesus's beatitude's sure sound like anything but happy, bliss, peaceful, blessed. In fact, they sound like the exact opposite. Antonyms I found for the word *beatitude* include *misery, sorrow, trouble,* and *upset.* Jesus's beatitudes sure sound like they should be called "the miseries" instead of the beatitudes.

Here's the thing. Here is what God has revealed to me through Mark's death that not many people will understand. During this journey of navigating through Mark's earthly death, God has become very real to me. I always believed but not like I do now. I have seen the face of God and have heard His voice in ways I never would have if I had not endured the pain and suffering of Mark's death. I have seen him show up in angels, in text messages, in peaceful moments that transcend all understanding. I have witnessed people's hearts opening to God to allow Him in when I have shared my journey. I have been brought to my knees, screaming, swearing, and surrendering to God because there was nowhere else to go and no one else to turn to, to fix my mess.

I met God in my darkest valley. I'm talking really met Him, heard Him, and felt immense comfort from Him, when I logically should not have felt comforted. Don't you see? We are blessed when "the miseries" hit because it is a prime time for us to allow God into our messes and meet Him for real. He shows Himself to be very real and very powerful. I've seen the work of the spiritual world, and it's very real. There is a very real battle between good and evil, and no one is immune to the attacks of the enemy.

My life has changed. Do I dare say for the better? How in the world is it possible to say my life has changed for the better because my husband died? It's not because he died. It's because God showed up through it. He has brought me to such a deep faith in Him that I wouldn't want any of those earthly blessings listed above if it meant I don't see and hear God. All those earthly blessings will be taken from you at some point in time while you are on this earth. We don't get to keep those. This world and everything in it are fleeting and temporary.

But God? Jesus? The kingdom of heaven and His promises? Those are eternal. Forever! Why do we store up for ourselves the things that wither away? Why do we not put more emphasis on the things of God—His kingdom, His instructions for how to treat others and how to live and how to glorify Him?

> Do not store up treasures here on earth, where moths eat them, and rust destroys them and where thieves break in and steal. Store your treasures in heaven, where moths and rust cannot destroy, and thieves do not break in and steal. Wherever your treasure is, there the desires of your heart will also be. (Matthew 6:19–21 NLT)

Will you still be able to say you are blessed when misery comes into your life? Will you find yourself more blessed than ever when your world is rocked to its core, and you can't do anything to change it? When misery comes (and it will at some point and in some form), will you read the beatitudes and understand that suffering will reveal the one true and real God in this world? Will you understand that suffering will bring you so close to God that you won't want it any other way? Will you understand that the blessing of drawing closer to God, seeking Him out, growing in your knowledge of Him, and becoming dependent on Him is really the only blessing we need? It's the only blessing that makes all our earthly blessings possible. It's the only blessing we can't afford to not have before we die. It's the only blessing that we can keep when we die. It's the only blessing that will carry over into our eternal life where it will be even better.

Although I now understand what Jesus's Beatitudes really mean and what it means to be truly blessed despite circumstances, I'd be dishonest if I didn't tell you I do have many moments when I fall away from these truths. A *lot* of times! After all, I am a human being, and I have many, many times when I don't feel blessed. I often feel robbed of the life I wanted. I wrestle with the concept of being cheated out of a lifelong marriage. My heart breaks often for my boys that they must grow up without their dad.

I often shout how totally unfair all of this is. Even though I know in the depths of my soul that the promises of God that I am discovering are true, that doesn't mean I don't have meltdowns. As a human being with human feelings and emotions, I have many momentary lapses of insanity over all of this. I have a finite mind and can only comprehend to a certain extent God's ways and plans. My thoughts are not His thoughts. His ways are wiser than mine. And when I forget this fact, scripture reminds me of this in Isaiah 55:8 NIV: "For my thoughts are not your thoughts, neither are your ways my ways, declares the Lord." He allows me to have my very real and raw human emotions but then always pulls me back in and reminds me of His goodness, sovereignty, and promises. That's the most awesome thing about the God I serve. I can be very real, raw, and honest with God about my feelings, and He welcomes it. He listens to it. He addresses it and then gives me peace about it.

As I write this, I notice that it is May 23, 2019. I'm only a couple of weeks away from my personal New Year. June 6 is quickly approaching, and I shake my head in disbelief that it will be nine years since Mark has died. Nine years! I will be entering my tenth year without him here on this earth. A decade! I have lived on for an entire decade.

I think about how Zane and Xavier were just two and five that horrible night when Mark was killed. As this school year comes to an end, it is hard for me to wrap my head around the fact that

Zane will be a freshman next year, and Xavier will start middle school. How in the world did I get here? How in the world has life continued for the last nine years? Somehow it has. It's been good, and it's been bad, with this last year being one of the worst years I've endured to date. The nightmare that became my life this past year is coming full circle, with, once again, God using it to teach me, change me, and mold me.

Being diagnosed with a panic disorder has taught me quite a few things. I've learned that my kids are totally awesome. They maintained honor roll status even when I was on complete autopilot and had no idea whatsoever what was going on in their little lives. I learned that I am awfully hard on myself and that I really am doing a phenomenal job raising my boys by myself.

I learned that the friends that I thought were trusted and true fell silent and that amazing support came from some very unexpected people. Not everyone is what they appear to be. A lot of fake is out there. I discovered that there are people who love me and love to be around me when I am strong and encouraging. However, when I broke, lost my strength and I needed the encouragement and support extended to me, those same people didn't know what to do with me, therefore, they fell silent.

I learned that I don't have the time, nor do I want to take the time, to devote energy and my heart to those who find me disposable. I've learned to forgive, let go, stay friendly and kind but to set boundaries. I've learned that becoming a widow with kids to raise by yourself is one of the most isolating positions a woman can find herself in.

I discovered that I don't really fit anywhere, and it's a whole different kind of widow with not much support. I learned that no matter how much time goes by, I will never get over something like Mark being killed under a camper. I move forward with stumbling blocks along the way. I learned that I have new goals, new thoughts, and new direction that was all brought on by what I persevered through this past year. I relearned that there is nothing that I can go through that Christ hasn't experienced Himself. He will never allow me to go through something so debilitating that He doesn't plan on using for great purpose and transformation of my being. I learned that with a lot of patience, a lot of commitment, a lot of open-mindedness, and a lot of new habits, I will feel the sunshine even through the rain.

CHAPTER 16

Moving Forward

Today is June 6, 2019—nine years since Mark has gone home. As I write this, I am at the place where Mark's soul was taken home. It is the most peaceful place in the world to me. Every year when I drive into this place, I sense that I have come home. This year is no different. In fact, it's even more peaceful. It's the day I celebrate making it through another year in this life, and it's the day I set a determination to keep moving forward.

I look around at the people that are here today, and I wonder. I wonder if they know what took place here on this day almost a decade ago. I wonder if my story is one of those stories people share without really knowing any of the details. I wonder if they tell the story that only happens to other people. I wonder if they tell *my* story. My story that is supposed to happen to other people. I look at two of the three women who were my rocks this past year that came with me today to the campground, and my heart is a grateful one, for God surely revealed who are the most trusted people in my life. They talked me through and out of crisis. They let me sob on their shoulders. They walked the block with me. They even witnessed me throwing up in my sink. They stayed all night with me because I couldn't stay alone. They sat on my front porch with me as I was nothing but a hollow shell of a person crying out to God to please rescue me.

They saw me at my worst, and today they see me at my best. This campground brings that out in me. Here's to another year of persevering. I had serious doubts that I would persevere this past year, but here I am, 90 percent Shannon again, praising God for His perfectly orchestrated death of Mark. Here I am, once again, feeling overwhelmed by the beauty of this place, the peace that transcends all understanding, and the faith that I believe in wholeheartedly.

Barely persevering this past year is what makes visiting the campground this year just as significant as that very first visit, one year after Mark died. I survived back then, and I survived my present circumstances, by the grace of God. His amazing power to restore me and reveal Himself through the suffering of this past year leaves me grateful, yet again, for the hardships He has allowed me to endure. I am thankful for the human beings He hand-selected to help bring me through. I am that much stronger than before. I am more determined than ever to push forward with new goals and a new agenda for my life. Happy New Year to me. I am entering my decade year. The journey keeps going.

So where does the journey go from here? What's next for me? Where am I today, and how am I doing? Well, for starters, I am still taking my medication. I still see my counselor once a month. I still practice the coping skills and strategies that I learned through therapy to control the anxiety and panic attacks. I continue to change any bad habits and replace them with new, good habits.

I continue to rid myself of toxic relationships by setting healthy boundaries and remembering to be friendly to all but to be true friends with the few. I continue to seek out opportunities that are healthy and that promote personal growth in my faith, in my wisdom, and for my overall well-being.

I've been saying lately that I am back to being about 90 percent Shannon again after this crazy year. However, I've come to recognize that I am back to 100 percent Shannon. I have a new facet to myself—that facet being susceptible to anxiety/panic attacks. Once again, God has transformed me, and being prone to anxiety and panic attacks is now part of me. At first thought, it sounds like a bad thing, but it is, in fact, the opposite. I truly believe that God has once again allowed something so horrible to enter my life, to only use it to grow me and transform me. He used it to complete this book. The book could not have been written without it. He is using it to guide me into the next phase of my journey.

I believe that God has me exactly where He needs and wants me to be. First and foremost, He continues to make it obvious that my top priority is being a mom to Zane and Xavier. With the passing of Father's Day this year, I've come to realize that, for whatever reason, God has called me to fill both roles of mother and father to my kids—and to two boys of all things! It's not because I'm that great or that strong. It's because He is that great and that strong to provide for what I lack in a "guy" or "father" role.

He knew I could handle it because I have Him. He provides when, honestly, no other man has really stepped up to take my boys under his wing to navigate through a boy's world view, so to speak. I find it mind-blowing that He chose me for such an awesome responsibility and honor. Those boys are all mine, and I love them so much. For some reason He chose me to be enough for my boys. Even in my weakest moments, I am enough. Even when I feel like I'm failing, I am enough. I am enough for them because I have Christ to guide me, and *that* is more than enough. When I feel weak, Christ shines through me the brightest. Second Corinthians 12:9–11 says it best:

> But he said to me, my grace is sufficient for you, for my power is made perfect in weakness. Therefore, I will boast all the more gladly in my weaknesses, so that Christ's power may rest on me. That is why, for Christ's sake, I delight in my weaknesses, in insults, in hardships, in persecutions, in difficulties. For when I am weak, then I am strong. (NIV)

As much as I hope that God's will for my life includes a significant other again, I feel in my heart that it isn't until later in life. It's after the boys are grown up and don't need me as much. I also believe that He has other things for me to accomplish and devote my time and energy to instead of a relationship with a man at this point. I would be lying if I said I don't care about meeting someone special again. Without a doubt, I want that for my life.

I don't necessarily ever want to be married again, but I'm not opposed to meeting someone. In fact, it would be nice. I also must be honest and say it's very frustrating that so many others who have lost spouses—men and women—seemed to have moved forward with someone in a shorter time than I have since I lost Mark. Even people who have divorced, seem to welcome new love into their lives. Here I am nine years later still "alone." It can leave me feeling as if there is something wrong with me or that I am surely doing something wrong.

However, I know those are only feelings and thoughts. Something I have learned through my therapy is that thoughts are just thoughts, and they aren't always true. Nothing is wrong with me. I was told by a good friend that not settling for someone just to have someone is a reflection of my character. I won't settle and I won't rush. It takes a long time to know somebody. So many people rush into serious relationships and are getting married in such a short time of knowing each other. I guess it's different for everyone, but that is so fast to me, and I can't do it.

So many people aren't willing to become friends and establish a real relationship anymore. I don't understand the rush, and if someone doesn't understand that, then they are not a match for me. I have had people make comments to me that they wish they could find me a good guy. While I appreciate that they are wanting happiness for me, I don't get the obsession with "finding someone." Why does that seem to be the end all? Why do people think being in a marriage is completeness? It's just not. I understand that I am totally speaking for myself, but a man is not something I need in my life. When and if the right one comes along, I will want him in my life. I will not allow anyone to put me down, discourage me, or manipulate me. I've been there with a few men I've dated since Mark has died.

I am thankful, however, for the wrong relationships that God ended. It taught me what *not* to stand for, and it helped pave my way to great independence and confidence in myself as a woman who can stand on her own two feet. It also taught me that I can't be in a relationship with someone who has no faith. I dated someone with no faith. His world was choas and negative. He was miserable and it brought me down. I'm not saying that someone has to believe everything that I do. I know I can get deep with my faith and I would never expect someone to think and believe identical to me. But a man will need to believe in God and have a spirituality to him. There has to be a common ground. The bottom line is this. If someone is meant to be in my life, he will be at the right time, in the right place. I can't force it. I would be miserable if I did.

Perhaps it may not be in God's plan for my life to connect with someone on that level again. If it's not, then who am I to force something that is not meant to be. It is far better to be without than with the wrong person just for the sake of having "someone." That's lonelier than being single. There are deeper and more significant things for me to focus on right now. Things that will deepen my faith and things that are important for my life, for the boys' lives, and for honoring God. God will fit all the pieces together, when they are meant to come together.

Publishing this book is the first goal that needs to be achieved. I need to do this for so many reasons. I need to for my boys. I need to for my healing. I need to so that others can understand how real the spiritual world is. I need to so that others can come to know the truth of who Christ is and what He has done for mankind. I need to do this for God. To give Him praise, honor, and the attention that He so deservingly should have.

I need to write this book so that it can encourage others who find themselves in similar situations. People need to understand that something like the tragedy I've endured is something you can never get over. It's been in the making for a long time—sitting stagnant for a while—waiting for the right time to emerge. Now is that time.

Something else I have been thinking about is going back to school to attain a master's degree in counseling. Having gone through this past year experiencing panic attacks, I now know firsthand how horrible it really is. I can't help but wonder how many other people are walking around in the same state that I was. How many people are hiding it so well that you would never know in a million years that they are stuck in panic-attack mode with physical ailments and fight-or-flight response? How many people are stuck in such a deep pit feeling hopeless, feeling embarrassed and ashamed with no end in sight?

I have now been there, and I want to help others. I want to talk to people, help people understand that mental health is as important as physical health. Just as physical ailments can manifest in your body, mental ailments can manifest in your brain. Your brain is no different than any other organ in your body. It can falter; it can hurt; it can go through trauma. It needs care, and no one should ever be ashamed to have to seek professional help for it.

I've become so intrigued with the brain—the science behind it all—that I'm constantly researching topics about it to understand it. I feel as if it's even more challenging to help "fix" the brain. When you break a bone, or get sick, for the most part, there is a plan of action to remedy the problem. But the brain is so different. It's so very fragile. It's where everything connects. It's where everything is processed. If your brain is "off," your whole body—physically and mentally—is off. It's home to all your memories and your life experiences and traumas.

It's all very fascinating to me, and I can become obsessed with wanting to learn about it. At this time, I have not yet investigated what I need to do to pursue a counseling career. I know it will be a lot of work. I know it will be time consuming. With my boys getting older, it may be the time to get started. Could the fact that God allowed anxiety and panic attacks to become a part of my life be His way of revealing to me that His plans for my life involve a second career of being a counselor? It may very well be. Nothing happens just to happen. He uses everything—*everything*—for a purpose.

When debilitating situations present themselves in your life, you can be sure that He is up to something. He is getting ready to change something in your life. Was that His intention all along, even when I was in the thick of panic this past fall/winter? Was He there all along, whispering in my ear, "Hold on! You'll see!"? What better way to turn the ashes of my past year into beauty than by leading me down a path to where I can truly help, comfort and change people for the better by providing TLC for their brain? It seems as if every time I turn around, the topics of anxiety, panic attacks, and mental health are bombarding me.

I come across random articles and books, and even find myself meeting and interacting with people who have had or who are currently experiencing exactly what I experienced this past year. I find myself sharing my experience of this past year with so many people who need to hear it. I find myself sharing what I learned in therapy because what I have learned has made a significant impact on me and in making new life habits.

I so much want others to know they don't have to feel embarrassed or ashamed for what is going on in their brains. I've experienced it hard core, and I came through it. I want others to learn what I learned—that with patience, commitment, change, open-mindedness, faith, and showing yourself love and kindness, they too, can get through it and come out stronger than before. I want to be able to provide faith, coping skills, compassion, therapy, and love to others.

It's so clear to me now that God didn't allow me to endure a panic disorder to punish me for some reason. He allowed it to mold me for the next chapter of my life. Time will tell. I must put one goal at a time into place, and the first goal is publishing this book. Perhaps goal number two will be attaining a counseling degree by the time I'm fifty. I have two years.

Speaking of God putting people in my path along the journey of last year, I met someone who I believe needed to meet me, and I needed to meet her. I advertised my boys' swing set on the Facebook marketplace. My boys have outgrown it, and I wanted it gone. So I advertised it as free if someone could come and disassemble it and haul it out of my backyard. This woman showed up at my house with some family members to get the swing set. She had all her kids with her, and I was making small talk with her. I'm not sure what was said to prompt her into sharing with me that her husband died two years ago. I then shared with her that my husband was killed nine years ago.

We exchanged our stories, and like my story, hers was unexpected and tragic as well. As we were talking, she looked at me at one point and asked, "Does it ever get any better?" What a question. I told her yes and no. This then opened the opportunity to share how almost a decade later, it came back hard core. I shared with her the panic attack horror I experienced. As I would tell her details, she would finish my sentences about feeling electric shock through your body, having memory issues, and walking around for days feeling like you were crawling out of your own skin. I was shocked. She had experience with exactly what I went through.

I don't know why I met this woman. Perhaps God knew she needed to meet a fellow widow left with kids to raise on her own. Maybe meeting me was God's way of showing her that she is not alone on this endeavor and that she, too, will prevail. Perhaps God knew I needed to meet a woman who could identify with what manifested in my life recently. Maybe meeting this woman was God's way of showing me how real and prevalent anxiety/panic attacks are and that I am not alone.

They hauled the swing set away, and we said goodbye. I have had no contact with her since and, honestly, don't really anticipate having any. I believe God handpicked her to receive a swing set that she would not otherwise have been able to afford. I believe God crossed our paths for a moment in time to provide comfort, strength, hope, and courage to two women who are walking similar paths with similar circumstances. A "God" incident for sure.

Talking about my boys' swing set recalls memories of those beginning months after Mark died. In fact, I got the swing set a couple of months after Mark died. I wanted to do something *big* for my boys and surprise them with the swing set all set up in the backyard, complete with a new pug puppy waiting to be found in the fort area of the swing set. (We still have our beloved Angel Puggy girl, by the way. We also brought another pug, Solomon, into the family three years later.)

Remember that Mark died in June, so it was warm those first few months after his death. After I would get the boys down for the night, I would go out and sit in the adult swing that came with the set and do a lot of pondering. I spent many hours sitting there talking to God, screaming at God, praying to God, and being silent with God. From time to time, Zane would join me out there. We had some deep discussions. Even at the age of five, Zane was wise beyond his years. He was asking me how Daddy got to go to heaven.

This opened such an opportunity for me to talk to Zane about who Jesus is and what He has done for us. I got to explain how Daddy invited Jesus into his life one day. I got to explain to Zane how Jesus dying on the cross is what makes it possible for Daddy to be in heaven, and for all of us to be there one day too.

He then asked me if heaven is the only place you can go to after you die. I then told him no. Your soul can also go to hell. If you are a believer in the Bible and in Christianity, you can't believe in heaven and not in hell. I was open and honest with my five-year-old that night. Zane then asked me about the differences between heaven and hell.

I was honest with him, and he then asked me how you decide which one you get to go to after you die. I explained that it all has to do with Jesus. Either you believe in Him and invite Him into your life, or you don't. Jesus is the way to heaven. Zane then asked me if you can change your mind and believe in Jesus after you die. I told him that no you can't. It's too late when you die. I told him that Jesus says, "But everyone who denies me here on earth, I will deny before my Father in Heaven" (Matthew 10:33 NLT). I explained to Zane how this verse says that Jesus wants us to acknowledge Him here on earth first, before we die. Zane at that point said, "Well, I want to have Jesus so that I can see Daddy again one day when I go to Heaven."

I prayed with my five-year-old right then and there. The foundation of Christ was laid down for Zane that summer night on that swing set. God's work in Zane's life began that night, all because of his father's death opening the opportunity to teach Zane the gospel of Jesus Christ. Again, Mark's tragic death was used for amazing good—the salvation of his son.

To this day, I still shake my head in disbelief sometimes. Every day I live with the surreal reality that Mark really did die. So many times I can't believe this is my life. No one goes into a marriage expecting it to end in "until death do us part" after only ten years of marriage. No one ever goes into a marriage expecting to be left to raise two young boys on their own. No one expects their husband to be killed, especially in such a tragic way. Who dies like that anyway? It's a crazy story. One you'll never hear again.

Mark always had to do things big, so why should his death be any different? When I see old videos of the four of us together, I can barely believe that was my life. It's as if I am watching someone else's life. I can hardly remember being a family of four. It's very odd to watch those old videos. It's painful, I suppose. But it's more bizarre, really. It doesn't feel like it was ever that way.

I often wonder what life would be like if Mark hadn't died. How different would the boys be? Would they be happier? Would they be more complete? Would I be a happier woman and mom? Would I be a good wife? Would Mark be a good husband/father? Would we have a good marriage? Would we even still be married? Would my faith be as strong as it is now? Would I understand what God says about suffering, pain, trials, and purpose? Would I have the deeper understanding of what Christ has done for me and for all? So many things to wonder about. However, it doesn't matter. It doesn't matter because this is the life God has planned for me on this earth.

We all have a plan for our lives. I can guarantee that God will show up and put a monkey wrench in your plans. It may not be as tragic as my monkey wrench, or it may be even more tragic than mine. Whatever the monkey wrench is, we have a choice in it. It's not a choice as to allow it or not, but it is a choice in how we are going to react to it, change from it, and proceed from it.

I have chosen to believe that God is in this life of mine 100 percent. I have chosen to believe that this world is not all there is. I have chosen to believe that Mark's tragic death serves great purpose. I have chosen to believe that there is great purpose to why the boys must grow up without their dad. This doesn't mean that I am happy all the time. This doesn't mean that I don't fall into pits of depression or have self-pity parties. Believe me, I do. I will continue to do so, I'm sure.

However, my overall belief system is always there even when I can momentarily abandon it. When I lose my happiness, my joy is still there. Joy is different than happiness. Happiness is based on external circumstances. Joy is based on the internal realization that Christ trumps anything horrible that happens in this earthly life. That joy persists when my happiness is fleeting. It's what I choose for my life. I choose God. I choose Jesus Christ. He chose me when I was that fifteen-year-old girl. It is impossible for me to ever be separated from Him. That is what sustains me and has brought me though the last ten years of life.

I realize that there may be people who read my book that do not share in my faith or have no faith at all. I sincerely hope that people of different faiths and belief systems read my book. I also hope that if you are someone who differs from me, that you will still be able to take away a message of hope, encouragement, and strength. If you are reading this, and you are struggling in life and having difficulty finding inner peace and healing from whatever life has thrown at you, I would then like to present a challenge to you.

Perhaps come out of your comfort zone and give this Jesus guy a chance. It certainly can't hurt you. If it does nothing for you, you won't be any worse off. And what if—just what if—sincerely opening your heart and inviting Him into your life does help you? What if putting in a sincere effort to seek Him and learn a little bit about Him does change your life for the better?

You have nothing to lose by investigating what true Christianity is and who in fact Jesus really is. It doesn't matter who you are. It doesn't matter where you are from, where you have been, or what you have done. It doesn't matter your race, your nationality, your culture, your gender, or your sexual identity. Jesus is for *everyone*! So, really, you have nothing to lose by at least checking Him out and giving Him a try. You may find that you gain the world. Not this earthly world, but the heavenly, eternal world where no pain, suffering, or sorrow exists. The world where my Mark now resides in a perfected presence. The world where I long to be.

EPILOGUE

It was only a trip to DC, so I'm sure this will sound ridiculous, but this past summer's road trip to DC was very significant. It was significant because it was the first big road trip that I packed my boys up for and ventured out alone, with just the three of us, since this past fall/winter. Anybody who knows me in the least knows that I have never been afraid to go anywhere with only the three of us. I'd pack us up and drive or fly to anywhere with no thought or concern about it.

However, as described in the previous chapters, the panic disorder and overwhelming irrational fears took over my whole life. I was afraid to leave the house. I could barely pick the boys up from school and take them to wherever they needed to be. It took every ounce of strength I could muster to do just that. Grocery shopping was a nightmare. Going anywhere was a nightmare. I had continuous feelings of crawling out of my skin with no relief for days on end. The only place I felt safe was in my bed. Although, I feared my bed at the same time because that is where I would experience the electric shock through my entire body that prevented any sleep for days. I was stuck. I was trapped in a world I never imagined myself in. I thought for sure that this was it. This was the rest of my life, and my existence would be a miserable, panic-stricken, and fearful one.

However, there I was, smack in the middle of Washington, DC, with only the boys and myself. Six to eight months earlier, I was trapped in my own head. Now, I was zipping along the crazy, congested, busy streets of DC on scooters with my boys leading the way through the city. I found myself again in this city. I found my independence again. I found my confidence again. I found my joy again. I found God again. I found the peace that transcends all understanding amid hectic Washington, DC.

In the middle of all that city noise, I heard God whisper my name. I heard Him say, "Look at you! I've got you. I always have." I felt His presence in the independence of my boys, who took it upon themselves to figure out how to get to everywhere in the city. I felt His presence in the cab ride to the Holocaust Museum. A Muslim cab driver drove a Christian woman and her kids to the Holocaust Museum. How amazing is that? I even had discussions about Islam and Christianity with the cab driver, who wished us a peaceful day. I felt God's presence at Arlington Cemetery where my heart was humbled and grateful for our great nation and all the heroes who died to make it so great.

I found my life again in DC this past summer. I found myself empowered, and I found myself at the end of the dark tunnel I had been in. The light poured back in. I really don't like the analogy of our lives going through seasons, but here I am using it. This past year was just a season. My season began to change the day I stepped foot in DC. The tough season that you are in will change too. Winter doesn't stay forever. The dark, gloomy days don't last forever. Whatever tough season you may find yourself in, keep the faith. Do what you must do to change things in your life. Do the therapy. Find the right medication. Make new habits and commit to them to see real, lasting changes. Seek out your most trusted peeps or ask God to reveal who those people are if you struggle with who to trust. He did that for me.

Before you know it, your body will stabilize out, you'll start to see purpose to the painful season, and you will smile again. You will be stronger. You will become thankful for enduring the roughest seasons. You will see how God will use it to lead you to new goals and to new opportunities. He will bring you to a deeper understanding of yourself and of Him. And, yes, you may even find yourself thankful for the death of your husband and for enduring a panic disorder.

I do love my life. I love the life He is mapping out for me. I love the amazing, perfectly orchestrated, beautiful, and tragic journey of it all. Having said that, please know that I still struggle. The truth is that I have many moments where I am not happy with my life at all. I fear that the panic attacks will come back full force. I often think far into the future and question what I will do when or if something happens.

I often miss Mark and want him back here with me. One of the worst things about losing Mark is when I remember a hilarious memory that's unique to the two of us, and he's not here for me to say to him, "Hey, remember when ..." I often can still get angry with God. I can still forget to pray or lack the desire to pray. I can often feel lonely, and I can have pity parties for myself.

The thing is, though, I always come through those rough moments. He brings me through. He reveals something, and it hits me deep inside, and I regain my peace and my faith. I often need to make a very conscience effort to remember all the miraculous revelations He has chosen to reveal to me over the course of the past ten years. I'll be honest, I sometimes forget and get selfish, because I want more "signs," if you will. I am human. I am broken. I am a work in progress and always will be until my time comes to enter the heavenly kingdom.

I'm learning to be patient with myself in these times. I'm learning to forgive myself and accept that I am not perfect, and I don't have to be because He is perfect for me. I only need to keep going forward. I only need to keep putting one foot in front of the other with total trust in Him that He is guiding my path one day at a time.

If you can identify with me at all, I pray that you will love your life too. I pray you will one day be able to see that it's all beautiful, even in the most horrid seasons. Keep your eyes and your heart open. Let Him reveal the splendor that will arise from what broke you down because He will. Just let Him. Give Him a chance. You have nothing to lose.

Printed in the United States
By Bookmasters